Up Front

Up Front

TEXT AND PICTURES BY

Bill Mauldin

NEW YORK: HENRY HOLT AND COMPANY

TO JEAN

Up Front

Up Front

MY BUSINESS is drawing, not writing, and this text is pretty much background for the drawings. It is not a book about my personal life or experiences. I don't think that would be very interesting to anyone but myself.

During the three years I spent in the 45th Division, I was certain that it was not only the best division in the army, but that it *was* the army. Since then I have kicked around in more than fifteen other divisions, and I have found that the men in each of them are convinced that their division is the best and the only division. That's good. Esprit is the thing that holds armies together. But it puts people who write about the army on the spot.

In order to do the right job, you'd have to mention six other outfits if you talked of one, and if you mention one battalion in a regiment, you're going to hear from the other two battalions, and the same with the companies. That is why I have mentioned specific units and persons as little as possible in this book.

*"You'll get over it, Joe. Oncet I wuz gonna write a book exposin'
the army after th' war myself."*

Since hanging around many different divisions, I've just about
come to the conclusion that when 15,000 men from 48 states are
put together in an outfit, their thinking and their actions are going to be pretty much like those of any other 15,000. Their efficiency and their accomplishments are altered to a certain extent

"Must be a tough objective. Th' old man says we're gonna have th' honor of liberatin' it."

by the abilities of their commanders, but the guys themselves are pretty much the same. I certainly have more affection for battered old outfits like the 34th, 3rd, 36th, 1st, 9th, 1st Armored, 2nd Armored, and my old 45th, which have been over here for two or three years and have fought through dozens of campaigns and

[3]

"Tell th' old man I'm sittin' up wit' two sick friends."

major battles. I think they and the old divisions in the Pacific have carried the major portion of the burden. And yet when you go through the line companies in those outfits you find, as I did in my old company, only four or five men who have been through the whole war. The rest have died or been crippled. Most of the men in those companies have been over about as long as the fellows in the newer divisions, and they are no different.

I would like to thank the people who encouraged me to draw army cartoons at a time when the gag man's conception of the army was one of mean ole sergeants and jeeps which jump over mountains. They not only encouraged me, but I know that they also backed me up when the drawings did not meet with unanimous approval from high brass. Many of these friends have been brass themselves, and I'm afraid that sometimes the drawings bit the hands that fed them. I wish there were some way to repay these people, and if this book were about my own army life, I might be able to make them feel better.

But it isn't that kind of book, and about all I can say is thanks to those I know about and many I don't know about—soldiers, officers, and others—because they encouraged me to draw pictures of an army full of blunders and efficiency, irritations and comradeship. But, most of all, full of men who are able to fight a ruthless war against ruthless enemies, and still grin at themselves.

I'm convinced that the infantry is the group in the army which gives more and gets less than anybody else. I draw pictures for and about the dogfaces because I know what their life is like and I understand their gripes. They don't get fancy pay, they know their food is the worst in the army because you can't whip up lemon pies or even hot soup at the front, and they know how much of the burden they bear.

But there are some people who object to writers and artists who consistently publicize one branch of the army. They say that such exclusive attention lowers the morale of the branches not publicized, and that it makes for self-pity in the branch whose troubles are aired. Maybe they are right. But I understand the infantry well enough to know that very few combat men are going to pity themselves more because their gripes are printed in a newspaper.

I felt I was in a pretty good spot to judge any effect the cartoons might have had on the morale of the rear echelon, since a lot

"Them wuz his exack words—'I envy th' way you dogfaces git first pick o' wimmen an' likker in towns.'"

of my time in the rear was spent pestering ordnance companies to work on my jeep, and bumming cigarettes and condensed milk from ration dumps. The guys back there never showed any inclination to lynch me—as a matter of fact, they had heard I was

[6]

"Ya won't have any trouble pickin' up our trail after th' first five miles, Joe."

in disfavor with a general, and when I came around for a new carburetor jet or more smokes they gave me stories about conditions in the rear, and ideas for cartoons.

I haven't tried to picture this war in a big, broad-minded way. I'm not old enough to understand what it's all about, and I'm not experienced enough to judge its failures and successes. My reactions are those of a young guy who has been exposed to some of it, and I try to put those reactions in my drawings. Since I'm a cartoonist, maybe I can be funny after the war, but nobody who has seen this war can be cute about it while it's going on. The only way I can try to be a little funny is to make something out of the humorous situations which come up even when you

[7]

don't think life could be any more miserable. It's pretty heavy humor, and it doesn't seem funny at all sometimes when you stop and think it over.

Since my drawings have been kicking around in some papers in the States, a lot of dogfaces over here have been very surprised, and so have I. Some of the drawings are meaningless even in Rome, Naples, or Paris. But the guys are glad and so am I, even if we are still surprised. If it means that people are interested in seeing how the dogfaces look at themselves, that's swell. If it means that people at home are beginning to understand these strange, mud-caked creatures who fight the war, and are beginning to understand their minds and their own type of humor, that's even more swell, because it means that the dogfaces themselves are beginning to be appreciated a little by their countrymen.

They are very different now. Don't let anybody tell you they aren't. They need a lot of people speaking for them and telling about them—not speaking for fancy bonuses and extra privileges. You can't pay in money for what they have done. They need people telling about them so that they will be taken back into their civilian lives and given a chance to be themselves again.

One of the foremost objections to a steady portrayal of the troubles and lives of combat infantrymen and those who work with them—medical aid men, combat engineers, artillery observers, and others—has been that these guys are going to feel that the nation owes them a living, and that they will become "social problems." This feeling has been so strong in some places that veteran combat men are looked at askance by worried and peaceable citizens. That's a sad thing for a guy who was sent off to war with a blare of patriotic music, and it's really not necessary.

[8]

"I'm d'most valooble man in d'third wave. Ever'body give me their cigarettes t' carry in me shirt pocket."

There will be a few problems, undoubtedly, because combat soldiers are made up of ordinary citizens—bricklayers, farmers, and musicians. There will be good ones and some bad ones. But the vast majority of combat men are going to be no problem at all. They are so damned sick and tired of having their noses

[9]

"Able Fox Five to Able Fox. I got a target but ya gotta be patient."

rubbed in a stinking war that their only ambition will be to forget it.

And there are so few men in the army who have really gone through hell that when they return they will be soaked up and absorbed by their various communities and they couldn't be problems if they wanted to. There are millions who have been inconvenienced. There are millions who have done a great and hard job. But so far there are only a few hundred thousand who have lived through misery, suffering, and death for endless 168-hour weeks and, as I said, they are going to be too tired and sick of it to bother anybody who might be worrying about their becoming problems.

They don't need pity, because you don't pity brave men—men who are brave because they fight while they are scared to death. They simply need bosses who will give them a little time to adjust their minds and their hands, and women who are faithful to them, and friends and families who stay by them until they are the same guys who left years ago. No set of laws or Bill of Rights for returning veterans of combat can do that job. Only their own people can do it. So it is very important that these people know and understand combat men.

Perhaps the American soldier in combat has an even tougher job than the combat soldiers of his allies. Most of his allies have lost their homes or had friends and relatives killed by the enemy. The threat to their countries and lives has been direct, immediate, and inescapable. The American has lost nothing to the Germans, so his war is being fought for more farfetched reasons.

He didn't learn to hate the Germans until he came over here. He didn't realize the immense threat that faced his nation until he saw how powerful and cruel and ruthless the German nation was. He learned that the Nazi is simply a symbol of the German people, as his father learned that the Kaiser was only a symbol. So now he hates Germans and he fights them, but the fact still remains that his brains and not his emotions are driving him.

[11]

"Run it up th' mountain agin, Joe. It ain't hot enough."

Many celebrities and self-appointed authorities have returned from quick tours of war zones (some of them getting within hearing distance of the shooting) and have put out their personal theories to batteries of photographers and reporters. Some say the American soldier is the same clean-cut young man who left

"Nonsense. S-2 reported that machine gun silenced hours ago. Stop wiggling your fingers at me."

his home; others say morale is sky-high at the front because everybody's face is shining for the great Cause.

They are wrong. The combat man isn't the same clean-cut lad because you don't fight a kraut by Marquis of Queensberry rules. You shoot him in the back, you blow him apart with mines,

*"Gimme my canteen back, Willie. I see ya soakin' yer
beard full."*

you kill or maim him the quickest and most effective way you
can with the least danger to yourself. He does the same to you.
He tricks you and cheats you, and if you don't beat him at his
own game you don't live to appreciate your own nobleness.

But you don't become a killer. No normal man who has smelled
and associated with death ever wants to see any more of it. In
fact, the only men who are even going to want to bloody noses
in a fist fight after this war will be those who want people to
think they were tough combat men, when they weren't. The
surest way to become a pacifist is to join the infantry.

I don't make the infantryman look noble, because he couldn't
look noble even if he tried. Still there is a certain nobility and

"I'd ruther dig. A movin' foxhole attracks th' eye."

dignity in combat soldiers and medical aid men with dirt in their ears. They are rough and their language gets coarse because they live a life stripped of convention and niceties. Their nobility and dignity come from the way they live unselfishly and risk their lives to help each other. They are normal people who have been put where they are, and whose actions and feelings have been molded by their circumstances. There are gentlemen and boors; intelligent ones and stupid ones; talented ones and inefficient ones. But when they are all together and they are fighting, despite their bitching and griping and goldbricking and mortal fear, they are facing cold steel and screaming lead and hard enemies, and they are advancing and beating the hell out of the opposition.

[15]

They wish to hell they were someplace else, and they wish to hell they would get relief. They wish to hell the mud was dry and they wish to hell their coffee was hot. They want to go home. But they stay in their wet holes and fight, and then they climb out and crawl through minefields and fight some more.

I know that the pictures in this book have offended some people, and I don't blame a lot of them. Some men in the army love their profession, and without those men to build the army we'd be in a sad fix indeed. Some of them I do blame, because the pictures don't offend their pride in their profession—they only puncture their stiff shirt fronts. I love to draw pictures that offend such guys, because it's fun to hear them squawk.

I'm sorry if I disturb the others, but they seldom complain. They know that if their men have a gripe, it is not good for them to sit in their holes and brood about it and work up steam. Men in combat are high-strung and excitable, and unimportant little things can upset them. If they blow that steam off a little bit, whether it is with stories or pictures or cartoons, then they feel better inside.

Not all colonels and generals and lieutenants are good. While the army is pretty efficient about making and breaking good and bad people, no organization of eight million is going to be perfect. Ours are not professional soldiers. They have recently come from a life where they could cuss and criticize their bosses and politicians at will. They realize that an army is held together with discipline, and they know they must have authority. They accept orders and restrictions, but because they are fundamentally democratic the insignia on the shoulders of their officers sometimes look a hell of a lot like chips.

[16]

"Awright, awright—it's a general! Ya wanna pass in review?"

I've been asked if I have a postwar plan for Joe and Willie. I do. Because Joe and Willie are very tired of the war they have been fighting for almost two years, I hope to take them home when it is over. While their buddies are readjusting themselves and trying to learn to be civilians again, Joe and Willie are going to do the same. While their buddies are trying to drown out the war in the far corner of a bar, Joe and Willie are going to drink with them. If their buddies find their girls have married somebody else, and if they have a hard time getting jobs back, and if they run into difficulties in the new, strange life of a free citizen, then Joe and Willie are going to do the same. And if they finally get settled and drop slowly into the happy obscurity of a humdrum job and a little wife and a houseful of kids, Joe and Willie will be happy to settle down too.

They might even shave and become respectable.

Soldiers are avid readers: some because they like to read and others because there is nothing else to do. Magazines and newspapers for which they subscribe arrive late and tattered, if they arrive at all. Half the magazines carry serial stories, which are a pain in the neck to the guys who start them and can't finish them as the magazines pass from hand to hand. Newspapers that have enough shreds left to be readable are so old that the only thing guys look for in their own home-town sheets is something about somebody they know. For that reason, the society sections of home papers probably get more attention than the feature pages. Joe's fiancée's picture is printed, showing her engaged to a war-plant worker, and he can pick out Aunt Suzy in the background of the picture taken at the annual tea party for the Quilting Bee Club.

Unfortunately, many papers at home burn soldiers up by printing the news just as it comes to them. If the campaign in Holland is taking up all the space, it burns the guys in Italy to read how "minor patrol action and comparative quiet continue on the Italian front, with no progress reported."

". . . so *Archibald* kissed her agin an' gently put her head on th' pillow. She gazed at him wit' half-shut eyes—tremblin' hard— don't forget to buy next week's installment at yer newsstand."

To a soldier in a hole, nothing is bigger or more vital to him than the war which is going on in the immediate vicinity of his hole. If nothing is happening to him, and he is able to relax that day, then it is a good war, no matter what is going on elsewhere.

[19]

"Th' hell this ain't th' most important hole in th' world. I'm in it."

But if things are rough, and he is sweating out a mortar barrage, and his best friend is killed on a patrol, then it is a rough war for him, and he does not consider it "comparatively quiet."

That situation can't be remedied much. Newspapers at home have to print the news as it appears on a world-wide scale, but if they would clamp down a little harder on their enthusiastic re-

"Fresh, spirited American troops, flushed with victory, are bring-
ing in thousands of hungry, ragged, battle-weary prisoners . . ."
(*News item*)

write men who love to describe "smashing armored columns," the
"ground forces sweeping ahead," "victorious, cheering armies,"
and "sullen supermen," they wouldn't be doing a bad job. A dogface gets just as tired advancing as he does retreating, and he

gets shot at both ways. After a few days of battle, the victorious Yank who has been sweeping ahead doesn't look any prettier than the sullen superman he captures.

It's tough that a lot of the blame for mistakes of the home-town newspapers is placed upon the war correspondents who cover the army, because they are the only newspapermen the soldiers see. Most war correspondents get the feel of the war after they have been around for a while, and some of them have seen more war than many combat soldiers.

There are bad war correspondents, and there are some who have been overseas for a long time without poking around to find out what the score is. A handful of newsmen stuck it out at Anzio from beginning to end, and they sent back some wonderful stories. They are the ones who can find real and honest stuff to write about in a war, regardless of whether or not that particular phase of the war is making headlines or getting them by-lines.

Will Lang from *Time* and *Life* became a familiar figure in several infantry regiments, and the story he wrote while trapped with a regiment at Salerno made him very popular with the guys. A sawed-off, freckle-faced reporter named Bob Vermillion voluntarily jumped with the paratroopers over Southern France, just so his story about them would be accurate. Ken Dixon, another reporter with his heart in the right place, roasted the pants off the general who commanded Naples, charging unfairness to combat troops. Ken got into some trouble over that, but because he lives with and writes about soldiers he is more interested in writing for them than for the generals.

Those three guys are among the civilian reporters to whom

"Why ya lookin' so sad? I got out of it okay."

the dogfaces are indebted. Their sole idea and purpose is to tell as much as they can about the war.

The mail is by far the most important reading matter that reaches soldiers overseas. This has had so much publicity that if some people aren't writing regularly to their guys in the war, it's because they don't want to. A common excuse at home seems to be that they aren't getting much mail from the guys here. The little lady says, "Okay, if the bum is going to sightsee around Europe and not bother to write, I just won't write him." Some guys do sightsee around Europe without bothering to write. Not the doggie. He doesn't do any sightseeing, and he doesn't have many opportunities to write. If the lady could see him scrawling on a V-mail blank in a dugout, by the light of a candle stuck with its own hot grease on his knee, she would change her way of thinking.

It's very hard to write interesting letters if you are in the infantry. About the only things you can talk about are what you are doing and where you are, and that's cut out by the censor. It's very hard to compose a letter that will pass the censors when you are tired and scared and disgusted with everything that's happening.

A lot of people aren't very smart when they write to a soldier. They complain about the gasoline shortage, or worry him or anger him in a hundred different ways which directly affect his efficiency and morale. Your feelings get touchy and explosive at the front. A man feels very fine fighting a war when his girl has just written that she is thinking that perhaps they made a mistake. He might figure: What the hell, the only thing I was living for was that I knew she would wait for me. He's going to feel pretty low and he might get a little careless because of it, at a place where he can't afford to be careless.

But considerate women have done far more to help their men than they may realize. A soldier's life revolves around his mail. Like many others, I've been able to follow my kid's progress

"My son. Five days old. Good-lookin' kid, ain't he?"

from the day he was born until now he is able to walk and talk a little, and although I have never seen him I know him very well. Jean has sent dozens of snapshots of herself and the little guy at different intervals, and it makes all the difference in the world.

Soldiers at the front read K-ration labels when the contents are listed on the package, just to be reading something. God knows they are familiar enough with the contents—right down to the last dextrose tablet. That puts *Stars and Stripes,* the only daily newspaper that reaches them with any regularity, in a pretty good spot.

Stars and Stripes would be an advertiser's dream, if it accepted advertisements. It has no big-scale competition, it reaches hundreds of thousands of readers, and it packs a lot of power because of that.

The original *Stars and Stripes* of World War I was started by a handful of privates and a sergeant or two, and, although they accumulated several officers along the way, it remained a soldiers' paper throughout the war. The *Stars and Stripes* of this war was started by a colonel. He built a chain of papers stretching from Casablanca to Rome, including Oran, Tunis, Algiers, Palermo, and Naples.

Although Egbert White was a colonel, he had been a private on the first *Stars and Stripes,* and I really think he tried to put out a newspaper for the troops in this war, and not an organ for the high brass. He staffed the papers with as many experienced newspapermen as he could find, and he kept reporters and correspondents in the field covering the troops. Many of his staff members had little journalistic experience before coming on the paper, and some of them came directly out of combat outfits. But all of them learned the business pretty well, and many of them have become expert newsmen.

When I was transferred to the paper in the early spring of 1944, I thought the old colonel was awfully timid. I had just come from the *45th Division News,* where we thought and wrote what we damned well pleased, just so we got a paper out. Because our paper was exclusively for combat soldiers, we didn't have to worry about hurting the feelings of high brass hats, who had never even heard of us. I couldn't understand the new arrangement, but as I learned a little from day to day I saw that the paper wasn't really timid—it just had to watch its step until it was established. It's established now, and for a long time has

"Another dang mouth to feed."

been printing a paper which upholds the reputation of the old *Stars and Stripes.*

The great majority of generals and authorities who see the sheet over here leave us strictly alone. There are, as in any big organization, some people who would like to see the editorial staff of the paper drawn and quartered, and there are still a few characters who make life uncomfortable sometimes, but we haven't lost a great deal of sleep over them. As far as I know, the paper has never had any trouble with field generals who actually command troops in combat. While the Italy edition of *Stars and Stripes* runs occasional pictures of General Mark Clark, who commands the Fifth Army in Italy, he gets no preference over anyone else. When Clark got Russia's highest foreign honor, the Order of Suvarov, he was given six lines of type on the last page of an eight-page edition. And he was probably surprised to get that much.

Sometimes the cartoon department of the paper got a little support from the higher brass, including Clark, although I never expected it, because the few cartoons I had done about generals had a definitely insubordinate air about them.

During that first winter in Italy, when *Stars and Stripes* printed letters from outraged combat soldiers in Naples, and when I did a few cartoons on the subject, the disturbance reached the ears of the deputy theater commander. He didn't see eye to eye with the paper and he forbade further distribution of some of the stuff I was doing. It wasn't his first or his last complaint about me, and when brass wearing three stars puts the clamps on you there is nothing much you can do about it. Yet right in the middle of the mess, a corps commander asked for the original of one of the drawings. I took the drawing to him, worrying a little about the fact that my uniform was mixed and my hair wasn't cut, and, besides, I wasn't accustomed to hobnobbing with corps commanders.

The first thing he asked me was, "How's your battle with the rear echelon progressing?" That staggered me. I replied that I

[28]

"That's okay, Joe—at least we can make bets."

had nothing against the rear echelon—only some of its generals —and that I was being accused by them of undermining somebody's morale.

He said, "When you start drawing pictures that don't get a few complaints, then you'd better quit, because you won't be doing anybody any good."

I felt a lot better.

I tried to stay completely away from stuff that had an editorial twist. The only editorializing you can do in the army is that which is approved by the army. I never could see any point in doing stuff that didn't show both sides. I kidded the rear echelon a little, but I also did an occasional drawing kidding the front about the unnecessary work it caused the ordnance and maintenance people. But I didn't do a drawing at all unless I

"Maybe th' sun's comin' up, Joe."

could work in a twist that made it at least slightly humorous.
Once I did get almost editorial—at the time when it looked as
though we weren't going to get to vote, because the bill was being
kicked around in Congress.

The only purely editorial cartoon I can remember was when
we were all bursting with enthusiasm and optimism about the
attempted assassination of Hitler. We felt that this was a sure
indication that Germany was cracking, and we would be home
by Christmas. I should have remembered we felt the same enthusiasm at Salerno when we first set foot on continental Europe
and began pushing inland. The Germans were disorganized after
the push started, and they all told us they surrendered because
they knew it would be over by Christmas and they didn't want
to get killed in the last days of the war.

"Let's grab dis one, Willie. He's packed wit' vitamins."

The only people who see my drawings before they appear in *Stars and Stripes* are the editor and the field press censor. Major Robert Neville, who runs the paper, was an enlisted man of long standing himself, and he lets his staff do its own thinking.

I never have trouble with the censor, because all he is worried about is preventing valuable information from falling into the hands of the Germans, who get the paper regularly through diplomatic channels and irregularly through Americans who are captured while carrying a copy. I do not draw pictures of new equipment until information about such equipment has been officially released, and, anyway, it would be hard in a cartoon to tell the Germans where the second battalion of the umpty-fifth regiment is going to attack. Except for that, I simply try to draw cartoons for the guys.

All that is as it should be. A soldiers' newspaper should recognize two restrictions—military security and common sense. Outside of that, it should devote itself solely to being a paper that will provide the soldiers with good news coverage and a safety valve to blow off their feelings about things.

We don't have to be indoctrinated or told there is a war on over here. We know there is a war on because we see it. We don't like it a darned bit, but you don't see many soldiers quitting, so fancy propaganda would be a little superfluous.

It's an accepted fact that you must be totalitarian in an army. The guys know that, but sometimes it chafes a little. That's why we do more bitching and groaning than any other army. And that's why it is a tremendous relief to get a little breath of democracy and freedom of speech into this atmosphere of corporals and generals and discipline and officers' latrines. It's a big relief even when it has to come from a little four-page newspaper.

While a guy at home is sweating over his income tax and Victory garden, a dogface somewhere is getting great joy out of wiggling his little finger. He does it just to see it move and to prove to himself that he is still alive and able to move it. Life

[32]

"I can't git no lower, Willie. Me buttons is in th' way."

is stripped down to bare essentials for him when he is living from minute to minute, wondering if each is his last. Because he is fundamentally no different from his countryman at home, he would probably be sweating just as hard over *his* income tax and Victory garden if *he* were home.

But now he has changed. His sense of humor has changed.

"Footprints! God, wotta monster!"

He can grin at gruesome jokes, like seeing a German get shot in the seat of his pants, and he will stare uncomprehendingly at fragile jokes in print which would have made him rock with laughter before.

Perhaps he will change back again when he returns, but never completely. If he is lucky, his memories of those sharp, bitter days will fade over the years into a hazy recollection of a period which was filled with homesickness and horror and dread and monotony, occasionally lifted and lighted by the gentle, humorous, and sometimes downright funny things that always go along with misery.

I'd like to talk about some of the things he will remember, and then I'd like to forget them myself.

Mud, for one, is a curse which seems to save itself for war. I'm sure Europe never got this muddy during peacetime. I'm equally sure that no mud in the world is so deep or sticky or wet as European mud. It doesn't even have an honest color like ordinary mud.

I made the drawing about the jeep driver and the foot infantry in the mud for a reason. Those guys who have had some infantry, and even those who have had to do a lot of walking in other branches, generally show it by the way they drive. If a man barrels past foot troops, splashing mud or squirting dust all over them because he doesn't bother to slow down—or if he shoots past a hitchhiker in the rain, with half his cozy truck cab empty—then he should spend a week or two learning how to use his feet, because he doesn't appreciate his job or he's just plain damned stupid.

Unfortunately, there are a lot of them in the army. I saw a big GI truck zoom past an infantry battalion in France, right after the rains began to fall. The driver spattered the troops pretty thoroughly—but they were getting used to being spattered, and they didn't say much. His truck bogged down half a mile up the road, and when the leading company caught up with him he had the unbelievable gall to ask them to push him out. They replied as only long-suffering infantrymen can reply. They shoved his face in the mud.

The worst thing about mud, outside of the fact that it keeps armies from advancing, is that it causes trench foot. There was a lot of it that first winter in Italy. The doggies found it difficult to keep their feet dry, and they had to stay in wet foxholes for days and weeks at a time. If they couldn't stand the pain they crawled out of their holes and stumbled and crawled (they

[35]

". . . I'll never splash mud on a dogface again (999). . . . I'll
never splash mud on a dogface again (1000). . . . Now will ya
help us push?"

couldn't walk) down the mountains until they reached the aid
station. Their shoes were cut off, and their feet swelled like bal-
loons. Sometimes the feet had to be amputated. But most often

"So I told Company K they'd just have to work out their replacement problem for themselves."

the men had to make their agonized way back up the mountain and crawl into their holes again because there were no replacements and the line had to be held.

Sometimes the replacement problem got fierce. Companies were down to thirty or forty men, but they managed to hold on somehow. It was worse than Valley Forge. I say that because conditions couldn't have been worse, and Washington's men didn't have to put up with murderous artillery and mortar fire.

I drew "Hit th' dirt, boys!" because I happened to be sliding down one of those mountains in Italy when I got nicked, and the only thing that saved me from most of the mortar shell was the fact that sliding down the hill made me as parallel to the

"Hit th' dirt, boys!"

earth as if I had been lying horizontally. Many hundreds weren't so lucky on the mountainsides.

This second winter in Italy is just as miserable. A lot of the guys have the new "shoe packs" which keep their feet reasonably dry, but that comfort is offset by the fact that this year they are getting more enemy artillery. The mountains are just as steep, the Germans just as tough, and the weather just as miserable. And those guys have been getting letters which say, "I'm so glad you're in Italy while the fighting is in France."

All the old divisions are tired—the outfits which fought in Africa and Sicily and Italy and God knows how many places in the Pacific. It doesn't take long to tire an outfit and many of the divisions that saw their first battle in France are undoubtedly

"I feel like a fugitive from th' law of averages."

feeling very fagged out right now. Like the men in the older
divisions, those men have seen actual war at first hand, seeing
their buddies killed day after day, trying to tell themselves that
they are different—*they* won't get it; but knowing deep inside
them that they *can* get it—those guys too know what real weariness of body, brain, and soul can be.

"I'm naked!"

I've tried to put their weariness and their looks into **Willie** and **Joe**, who started with them and are getting tired with them. I tried shaving Willie once, but he just didn't look right, so the next day he had his beard back. I've tried two or three times to bring in replacements, but I've discovered that I have been here too long myself now to understand the feelings or reactions of a replacement fresh from home.

I've seen too much of the army to be funny about first sergeants and corporals, and I've seen too much of the war to be cute and fill it with funny characters.

I wish I could have written this book during my first six months overseas. Then all things in war make a vivid impression on you because they are all new to you. You can describe sorrow-

"How ya gonna find out if they're fresh troops if ya don't wake 'em up an' ask 'em?"

ful things and funny things with great enthusiasm, and in such a way that people will understand you. But, as the months go on and you see more of war, the little things that are so vivid at first become routine. I haven't tried to describe the activities of the infantry and its weapons because everybody has learned how a BAR man covers a light machine-gunner. I don't describe dead guys being buried in bloody bed sacks because I can't imagine anyone who has not seen it so often that his mind has become adjusted to it. I've simply described some of the feelings which the dogfaces have about different things, and to describe these things I have drawn cartoons about Willie and Joe.

Willie and Joe aren't at all clever. They aren't even good cartoon characters, because they have similar features which are

[41]

"We just landed. Do you know any good war stories?"

distinguishable only by their different noses. Willie has a big nose and Joe has a little one. The bags under their eyes and the dirt in their ears are so similar that few people know which is Willie and which is Joe.

True, Joe and Willie don't look much like the cream of young American manhood which was sent overseas in the infantry. Neither of them is boyish, although neither is aged. Joe is in his early twenties and Willie is in his early thirties—pretty average ages for the infantry. While they are no compliment to young American manhood's good looks, their expressions are those of infantry soldiers who have been in the war for a couple of years.

Look at an infantryman's eyes and you can tell how much war he has seen. Look at his actions in a bar and listen to his talk and you can also tell how much he has seen. If he is cocky and troublesome, and talks about how many battles he's fought and how much blood he has spilled, and if he goes around looking for a fight and depending upon his uniform to get him extra-special privileges, then he has not had it. If he is looking very weary and resigned to the fact that he is probably going to die before it is over, and if he has a deep, almost hopeless desire to go home and forget it all; if he looks with dull, uncomprehending eyes at the fresh-faced kid who is talking about the joys of battle and killing Germans, then he comes from the same infantry as Joe and Willie.

I've made it sound as if the only infantry is the kind that spends its time being miserable and scared in foxholes. There are other kinds. There are those who like it and those who have reasons of their own for wanting it. I know two of these notable exceptions: a swamp hunter from Georgia and an exiled baron from Prussia.

The swamp hunter once killed eight krauts with one clip from his M-1 rifle. He loves to go on patrol, all alone, with a rifle, a Luger pistol, a knife, plenty of ammunition, and half a dozen grenades hung to his belt by their safety rings, so he can pluck them and throw them like ripe tomatoes. The fact that hanging grenades by their rings is not a good way to live to a respectable old age doesn't bother him at all. In fact, he tells with great relish how one came loose while he was creeping around a German position, and how it exploded under his feet, kicking his legs up in the air, but leaving him miraculously unscratched. He once saved his entire company by sheer guts, and he has been decorated several times. He says war is just like swamp hunting.

The Prussian is a wild character who received a battlefield

[43]

"I need a couple guys what don't owe me no money fer a little routine patrol."

promotion to lieutenant, after saving a patrol and the officer who commanded it from annihilation. He is famed far and wide for leading his own patrols fantastic distances through enemy lines. He admits he gets scared, but his hatred for the Germans is so intense that he keeps it up. He has been wounded a number of times. His favorite weapon is the tommy gun, although he used a carbine once to shoot a German officer through the throat, and then almost wept because he had shattered the officer's fine binoculars. He has saved many lives and has got a lot of valuable information by the simple process of sneaking into a darkened kraut command post at night, demanding to know the plans and situation in his arrogant Prussian voice, and then sneaking back to our side again.

I know of another guy—a former racketeer's bodyguard—who once found two Germans sleeping together to keep warm, remembered an old Ghoum trick, and slit the throat of one, leaving the other alive so he would wake up and see his bunkmate the next morning. Most of the doggies thought it was a good stunt, and it kept the Germans in his sector in a state of uproar and terror for several days.

The army couldn't get along without soldiers like that. They provide wonderful stories, they inspire their comrades to greater feats of arms, and they do a lot to make Jerry fear the American army.

Joe and Willie, however, come from the other infantry—the great numbers of men who stay and sweat in the foxholes that give their more courageous brethren claustrophobia. They go on patrol when patrols are called for, and they don't shirk hazards, because they don't want to let their buddies down. The army couldn't get along without them, either. Although it needs men to do the daring deeds, it also needs men who have the quiet courage to stick in their foxholes and fight and kill even though they hate killing and are scared to death while doing it.

[45]

"She must be very purty. Th' whole column is wheezin' at her."

Many people who read and speak of battle and noise and excitement and death forget one of the worst things about a war—its monotony. That is the thing that gets everyone—combat soldier and rear echelon alike.

The "hurry up and wait" system which seems to prevail in every army (double time to the assembly area and wait two hours for the trucks—drive like hell to the docks and wait two days for the ship—fall out at four in the morning to stand an inspection which doesn't come off until late afternoon), that's one of the things that make war tough. The endless marches that carry you on and on and yet never seem to get you anyplace—the automatic drag of one foot as it places itself in front of the other without any prompting from your dulled brain, and the

"I'm depending on you old men to be a steadying influence for the replacements."

unutterable relief as you sink down for a ten-minute break, spoiled by the knowledge that you'll have to get up and go again —the never-ending monotony of days and weeks and months and years of bad weather and wet clothes and no mail—all this sends as many men into the psychopathic wards as does battle fatigue.

Like fraternity brothers who have had a tough initiation, many of the old-timers over here are ornery enough to kid replacements who begin to feel pretty miserable and homesick after six months. "The first year is the worst," the old-timers say. "The second year isn't so bad, and by the time you begin your third year overseas you are almost used to it."

But it ain't true, brother; it ain't true.

My dad used to tell me how in the First World War German and American outfits, living a miserable, monotonous life in the trenches, used to get acquainted with each other. That hasn't happened much in this war, but during the awful winters in Italy things often slowed down to a dead stop, and after a while lonely guys would connect their foxholes and have real old-fashioned trenches. Most of the trenches were pretty well surrounded with barbed wire and minefields, so in many ways it was just like the other war.

The opposing sides often spoke to each other, but seldom in brotherly tones. It was a favorite trick to confuse the enemy by yapping at him in his own tongue. Both sides did it, sometimes quite successfully. Once I heard a funny exchange between a Westerner and a German in the mountains above Venafro. The American had a machine-gun position on top of a hill, and the kraut was a sniper, about fifty yards down the slope. They were well protected, and had been in those positions for many days. Both had cooties, both had trench foot, and each had an intense dislike for the other.

An Italian division was supposed to move into the line near by. The Nazis, having had experience with the Italians when they were fighting on the German side, liked this new idea very much.

"Wot kind of voices—Brooklyn or guttural?"

The Americans, who had seen the Italians as German allies, were not cheered by the prospect.

"How do you like your new ally?" yelled the German to the American in passable English.

"You kin have 'em back," said our guy, having come from a region where diplomacy bows to honesty.

"We don't want them," shouted Jerry, and he lobbed a grenade up the hill. It fell far short.

The American spattered the sniper's rocks with a burst.

"Swine!" jeered the German.

"Horse's ass!" snorted the American, and all was quiet again.

The Germans often accuse us of being low plagiarists when it comes to music, and that we cannot deny. Our musical geniuses at home never did get around to working up a good, honest, acceptable war song, and so they forced us to share "Lili Marlene" with the enemy. Even if we did get it from the krauts it's a beautiful song, and the only redeeming thing is the rumor kicking around that "Lili" is an ancient French song, stolen by the Germans. It may not be true, but we like to believe it.

"Lili" got a couple of artillerymen in trouble in France. They were singing it at a bar the day after this particular town had been taken. Some local partisans came over and told them to shut the hell up. The guys understood, apologized, and bought drinks all around.

I read someplace that the American boy is not capable of hate. Maybe we don't share the deep, traditional hatred of the French or the Poles or the Yugoslavs toward the krauts, but you can't have friends killed without hating the men who did it. It makes the dogfaces sick to read articles by people who say, "It isn't the Germans, it's the Nazis." Our army has seen few actual *Nazis,* except when they threw in special SS divisions. We have seen the Germans—the youth and the men and the husbands and the fathers of Germany, and we know them for a ruthless, cold, cruel, and powerful enemy.

"Th' krauts ain't followin' ya so good on 'Lili Marlene' tonight, Joe. Ya think maybe somethin' happened to their tenor?"

When our guys cringe under an 88 barrage, you don't hear them say, "Those dirty Nazis." You hear them say, "Those goddam krauts." Because our men soon learn to be more or less professional fighters at the front, they have a deep respect for the

"Let B Comp'ny go in. They ain't been kissed yet."

German's ability to wage war. You may hear a doggie call a German a skunk, but he'll never say he's not good.

The very professionalism of the krauts which makes the American infantryman respect the German infantryman also makes him hate the German's guts even more. The dogface is quite human about things, and he hates and doesn't understand a man who can, under orders, put every human emotion aside, as the Germans can and do.

Some very unfortunate rumors have drifted over here, from time to time, about the treatment of prisoners of war in America. While the guys here realize it is much more economical to haul krauts back to the States on empty ships, rather than use crowded shipping space to send food over here for them, there is a natural resentment because the enemy gets a privilege that is denied those who fight him. He gets to go back and breathe the air of God's country, even if it is in a prison camp. That's a very human and natural feeling, which can be fully understood only if you have experienced the deep longing for your home country that we have felt here.

Since the Germans have many of our own men, and because we are supposed to be a civilized people, we certainly want the krauts to be treated within the rules, but only within the rules.

There is no indication that the rumors were true, but whoever started them was guilty of a criminal thing. One of the rumors was that some Americans gave a dance for Italian POWs. Another was that a German camp had struck for higher wages for the labor they were forced to do. While most of the soldiers here know that such stuff simply comes from the rumor mills, there are always some who are willing to believe rumors, and there are many who fear that the American people will go soft with the prisoners. Even some American soldiers are lenient with them; but not those who capture them. They have to fight Germans, and they do not like the herrenvolk. Because, as I said, many of them have friends whom the Germans have captured, they don't object to taking krauts alive. But they certainly feel that the prisoners, who should thank God and not their Fuehrer that they

*"Hell. When they run we try to ketch 'em. When we
ketch 'em we try to make 'em run."*

have been permitted to remain alive and breathe air which would
be much purer without their presence, should remember that they
are enemies.

The Germans prefer to surrender to Americans rather than to
some Europeans, because they know they will be treated fairly.
Being Germans they take advantage of this sometimes. I
watched a crippled FFI man working the hell out of a detail of
German prisoners at the docks of Marseilles. He was not abusing
them; he was simply making certain their hands got calloused.
He had been crippled by the Germans and they had wrecked the
docks, so his heart was in his work. Then an American sergeant,
who had the air of a man freshly arrived in Europe, strolled past

"I made it. I owe ya another fifty bucks."

and stared at the prisoners. Immediately they began groaning and limping and looking sick, weary, and picked-on. The sergeant stopped the work and gave each man a cigarette. The Frenchman stood and watched him do it and then limped away disgustedly. The American turned his back for a moment, and the entire detail of krauts grinned at each other.

I wouldn't be surprised if a German corporal named Schicklgruber received an American cigarette under similar conditions twenty-six years ago.

Friends in war are different in many ways from friends in peacetime. You depend upon friends in war much more.

The infantrymen can't live without friends. That forces them

"Why th' hell couldn't you have been born a beautiful woman?"

to be pretty good people and that's the reason men at the front seem so much simpler and more generous than others. They kid each other unmercifully—sometimes in ways that would seem a little ribald to the uninitiated.

For instance, there's the young guy who got married two

weeks before shipping out, has been overseas two years, and is desperately homesick. Some other guy will say to him:

"You wanna go home? Hell, you found a home in the army. You got your first pair of shoes and your first square meal in the army. You're living a clean, healthy, outdoor life, and you want to go back and be henpecked."

He keeps up this apparently heartless tirade until the victim heaves a big rock at him and feels better. But it isn't heartless, because only a man who is terribly homesick himself would dare to say a thing like that. He isn't just pouring it on the other guy —he's trying to kid *himself* into feeling better.

When you lose a friend you have an overpowering desire to go back home and yell in everybody's ear, "This guy was killed fighting for you. Don't forget him—ever. Keep him in your mind when you wake up in the morning and when you go to bed at night. Don't think of him as the statistic which changes 38,788 casualties to 38,789. Think of him as a guy who wanted to live every bit as much as you do. Don't let him be just one of 'Our Brave Boys' from the old home town, to whom a marble monument is erected in the city park, and a civic-minded lady calls the newspaper ten years later and wants to know why that 'unsightly stone' isn't removed."

I've lost friends who were ordinary people and just wanted to live and raise a family and pay their taxes and cuss the politicians. I've also lost friends who had brilliant futures. Gregor Duncan, one of the finest and most promising artists I've ever known, was killed at Anzio while making sketches for *Stars and Stripes*. It's a pretty tough kick in the stomach when you realize what people like Greg could have done if they had lived. It's one of the costs of the war we don't often consider.

[57]

Those thoughts are deep in us, and we don't talk about them much.

While men in combat outfits kid each other around, they have a sort of family complex about it. No outsiders may join. Anybody who does a dangerous job in this war has his own particular kind of kidding among his own friends, and sometimes it doesn't even sound like kidding. Bomber crews and paratroopers and infantry squads are about the same in that respect. If a stranger comes up to a group of them when they are bulling, they ignore him. If he takes it upon himself to laugh at something funny they have said, they freeze their expressions, turn slowly around, stare at him until his stature has shrunk to about four inches and he slinks away, and then they go back to their kidding again.

It's like a group of prosperous businessmen telling a risqué joke and then glaring at the waiter who joins in the guffaws. Combat people are an exclusive set, and if they want to be that way, it is their privilege. They certainly earn it. New men in outfits have to work their way in slowly, but they are eventually accepted. Sometimes they have to change some of their ways of living. An introvert or a recluse is not going to last long in combat without friends, so he learns to come out of his shell. Once he has "arrived" he is pretty proud of his clique, and he in turn is chilly toward outsiders.

That's why, during some of the worst periods in Italy, many guys who had a chance to hang around a town for a few days after being discharged from a hospital where they had recovered from wounds, with nobody the wiser, didn't take advantage of it. They weren't eager to get back up and get in the war, by any means, and many of them did hang around a few days. But those

"Joe, yestiddy ya saved my life an' I swore I'd pay ya back. Here's my last pair of dry socks."

who did hang around didn't feel exactly right about it, and those who went right back did it for a very simple reason—not because they felt that their presence was going to make a lot of difference in the big scheme of the war, and not to uphold the traditions

"We'll report we made contack wit' th' enemy an' walked to our objective."

of the umpteenth regiment. A lot of guys don't know the name of their regimental commander. They went back because they knew their companies were very shorthanded, and they were sure that if somebody else in their own squad or section were in their own shoes, and the situation were reversed, those friends would come back to make the load lighter on *them.*

That kind of friendship and spirit is a lot more genuine and sincere and valuable than all the "war aims" and indoctrination in the world. I think the wise officers who command these guys realize that. They don't tolerate bootlicking or petty politicking. Even though, as in the case of the guys alibiing for each other because of the smashed jeep, the officer will be sore as hell, he will have more respect for them than if one of them had come to him privately and whispered in his ear, "Joe did it."

There is surprisingly little bickering and jealousy in combat outfits. There might be a little between the company cooks or the supply sergeant and the company clerk, but the more action anybody sees the less spiteful he is toward those around him.

If a man is up for a medal, his friends are so willing to be witnesses that sometimes they must be cross-examined to make sure they are not crediting him with three knocked-out machine guns instead of one. They fight together, argue together, work together, stick together if one is in trouble, and that's a very big reason why infantry guys win wars.

If one man out of a platoon gets a six-hour pass to go back to a town, he will have a good time for himself, of course. It's expected of him. But he will come back with a load of cognac for those who didn't get to go. Guys hitchhike many miles to visit their friends who are in hospitals, and sometimes they will go over to another division to see an old buddy if they have a little time on their hands.

If a man in a rifle squad gets a chance to go home on rotation, his friends congratulate him, tell him they wish to hell they were going themselves, but, as long as they can't, they give him their families' phone numbers, and they wish him a fare-thee-well and join him in the fond hope that he never has to go overseas again. While they envy him like the devil, they aren't low-down about it. The man who goes home carries a huge list of telephone numbers and addresses, and he makes all the calls and writes all the letters, even though it often costs him considerable time and expense during his own precious few days.

Very few of them shoot off their mouths about their own hero-

"I brang ya a chaser fer all that plasma, Joe."

ism when the inevitable reporter from the home-town paper comes around to see them. They are thinking of their friends who are still having troubles, and how the article will be read by their outfits when the clippings reach them. I've seen few clippings come over here about men who have had a really tough war, and even fewer pictures of them displaying gory souvenirs.

"Did ya ever see so many furriners, Joe?"

Of course, there are misfits who just can't make friends or who are just plain ornery, but they depart sooner or later. If something doesn't happen to them during battle, they blow their tops or they just leave when there is an opportunity. But you will seldom find a misfit who has been in an outfit more than a few months.

I'm not equipped to talk about Europe because I don't know a darned thing about it. My impressions are simply reactions to what I have seen, and all I can do is offer them as explanations for some of the drawings I made about the experiences soldiers have had with civilians here and there.

While most guys over here swear heartily at the people who

always seem to be trying to take advantage of us, we all have to admit that deflating the GI pocketbook is not an activity peculiar to Europe. We still have dim memories of days long ago when shops and restaurants in some American towns kept double price lists for soldiers and civilians, and those of us who had wives can't forget rooming houses whose proprietors hung out "Soldiers' Families Welcome" signs, and then stuck us for all our monthly pay.

Those of us who have spent a long time in Sicily and Italy are more amazed every day that such a run-down country could have had the audacity to declare war on anyone, even with the backing of the krauts.

The dogfaces over here have pretty mixed feelings as far as Italy is concerned. A lot of them—but not as many as there used to be—remember that some of their best friends were killed by Italians, and many of our allies can't forget that Italy caused them some grief. I don't belong to that group, even though the first enemies I saw were Italians. You can't work up a good hate against soldiers who are surrendering to you so fast you have to take them by appointment. But the average dogface feels dreadfully sorry for these poor trampled wretches, and wants to beat his brains out doing something for them. I don't belong too strongly to that group, either. The Italians haven't given me a chance to give them anything; they have stolen everything I own except the fillings in my teeth.

Italy reminds a guy of a dog hit by an automobile because it ran out and tried to bite the tires. You can't just leave the critter there to die, but you remember that you wouldn't have run over it if it had stayed on the sidewalk. There is no doubt

"Go ahead, Joe. If ya don't bust it ya'll worry about it all night."

that the Italians are paying a stiff price for their past sins. The country looks as if a giant rake had gone over it from end to end, and when you have been going along with the rake you wonder that there is anything left at all.

The doggies become accustomed to the abject poverty and hunger of the Italian refugees who stream out of towns which

The Prince and the Pauper.

are being fought over, and who hang around bivouac areas, but no dogface ever becomes hardened to it. Also, they get awfully tired of hearing everybody—Fascists, ex-Fascists or non-Fascists —wail about how Mussolini made them do it. Their pity is often strained by the way the Italians seem to wait for somebody else to do something for them, but in spite of the fact that the Italians consider the Americans a gravy train which came to bring them pretty things to eat, the doggies still pity them.

It would take a pretty tough guy not to feel his heart go out to the shivering, little six-year-old squeaker who stands barefoot in the mud, holding a big tin bucket so the dogface can empty his mess kit into it. Many soldiers, veterans of the Italy campaign and thousands of similar buckets, still go back and sweat

"It's a habit Joe picked up in th' city."

out the mess line for an extra chop and hunk of bread for those little kids.

But there is a big difference between the ragged, miserable infantryman who waits with his mess kit, and the ragged, miserable civilian who waits with his bucket. The doggie knows where

"Tell him to look at th' bright side of things, Willie. His trees is pruned, his ground is plowed up, an' his house is air-conditioned."

his next meal is coming from. That makes him a very rich man in this land where hunger is so fierce it makes animals out of respectable old ladies who should be wearing cameos and having tea parties instead of fighting one another savagely for a soldier's scraps.

I think that's where the guys direct their sympathies: toward the old people and the little kids, who certainly never had much to say about the sacking of Greece and the invasion of Ethiopia. The men of Italy—the strapping young guys who didn't realize their own country's weakness—evidently sense this, because they don't come around the mess lines. They steal jeep parts instead.

It hits the doggies to see a man staring glassily at the shambles of the home he spent his life building, and they would like to be able to comfort him. Perhaps they feel that way because they realize more and more how lucky our own country is to have escaped all this. It chills a man to see a young girl, with a haunted, hopeless expression in her eyes and a squalling baby which must go on squalling because she is hungry and has no milk for it. Not only does he pity her, but he thinks that this could possibly have happened to his own sister or his wife. He realizes it even more when he considers how near the Germans were to victory when he started fighting them. Thoughts like that sometimes keep guys going.

The medical corps has probably done more to endear our army to civilians in stricken areas of Europe than the high-powered agencies which came over with that task in mind.

No one will ever know how many French, Sicilian, and Italian kids will go through life bearing the first names of the doctors who, in their own spare time when they needed rest badly, made the deliveries in chilly stables and leaking aid tents. Nobody ever hesitates to apply to our medics for aid; and the medics, who manage to keep their profession pretty high above the selfish motives which cause wars, usually try to help them.

Nearly everyone who has hung around a battalion aid station

[69]

"It's twins."

in a zone where there are refugees has seen the civilians with banged-up ribs or nicks from stray bullets and shell fragments coming around for treatment. But the most beautiful sight of all is the man you will occasionally see who crumples and un-crumples his battered hat as he paces up and down in front of the aid station with the same worried air, and for the same reason, as a man pacing the tiled floor of a maternity ward at home. The only difference is that here the expectant papa has no cigarettes to smoke.

Most people in Italy and Sicily gave us a rousing welcome in all their towns and cities, but nowhere was there such excitement as in Rome. We got awful cynical about it, because the enthusi-

"Don't look at me, lady. I didn't do it."

asm seemed to stop, and the complaints seemed to start, twenty-four hours after everybody was kissing everybody else. When were we going to bring shoes and food and clothes and phonograph records? Who was going to pay for Uncle Antonio's bombed vino shop, and why did we have to shell Aunt Amelia's ristorante?

They beefed most about the bombs. Those really did tear hell out of things, and somehow we never did have the heart to ask the Italians when they were going to pay for the damage *they* did in the war.

Some of the housewives were downright furious as they poked through the rubble of what had been their parlors. They seemed to forget that their town was full of German tanks and German

"Are you seeking a company of infantry, mon capitaine?"

supplies; instead, they regarded our fliers as a bunch of irresponsible kids with itchy bombsights.

Europeans have been hardened to centuries of war and invasion and they seem to know what to expect from soldiers. While

I have a natural preference for my own countrymen, the contact I have had with other allied troops leads me to believe that soldiers are pretty much alike, no matter where they come from. They all want to go home more than anything else, and they all feel a certain freedom from the conventions they would observe in their own countries. In fact, about the only factors that decide a soldier's conduct in foreign lands are army regulations, his own conscience, and the way he is treated by civilians.

I've found this to be true all through the army. In the American towns where my division was stationed from time to time during its training, the size of the MP force which policed the town was regulated by how much the local inhabitants tried to gyp us.

If the people were warm and hospitable, as they were in many places, the few drunken soldiers who appeared on the streets were taken in hand by their buddies before anybody saw them. In the towns where soldiers were not only disliked, but actually treated with hostility (and there were plenty of those towns too), we didn't interfere with our more boisterous brethren as they roamed the midnight streets looking for windows to break.

The very guys who caroused so wildly on the streets of Naples behaved themselves pretty well in many towns in France where we were welcomed openly and sincerely.

We are swindled unmercifully everywhere we go; we've learned to take it for granted. But a lot of the blame is our own. If we find a barbershop where the price equals six cents in American money, we plop down what amounts to fifty cents in tattered European currency. When our change is counted out to us in even more tattered bills—some worth as little as one cent—

we tell the barber to keep the change. We'd have paid that price in America, and besides, we hate to have wads of the stuff sticking between our fingers every time we reach into our pockets for a cigarette.

After two or three dogfaces have repeated this performance, the barber decides the stories he has heard about all Americans owning oil wells are true, and the price goes up to fifty cents. Along comes a Canadian, whose government allows him about ten dollars per month and banks the rest for his return, and when the barber tries to soak *him* fifty cents the Canadian tears the shop apart.

All this leads the confused barber to believe that the Canadian is a tightwad and the American is a rich fool.

I've done many drawings of wrecked buildings. Shattered towns and bomb-blasted houses are constant reminders of the war, long after the dead are buried.

There's something very ghostlike about a wall standing in the moonlight in the midst of a pile of broken rubble and staring at you with its single unblinking eye, where a window used to be. There's an awful lot of that in Italy, and it is going to haunt those people for years.

You can usually tell what kind of fighting went on in a town, and how much was necessary to take it, by the wreckage that remains. If the buildings are fairly intact, with only broken windows, doors, and pocked walls, it was a quick, hand-to-hand street fight with small arms and grenades and perhaps a mortar or two.

If most of the walls are still standing, but the roofs have gaping holes, and many rooms are shattered, then the entry was

"It ain't right to go around leanin' on churches, Joe."

preceded by an artillery barrage. If some of the holes are in the slopes of the roofs facing the retreating enemy, then he gave the town a plastering after he left.

But if there isn't much town left at all, then planes have been around. Bombs sort of lift things up in the air and drop them in a heap. Even the enormous sheet-metal doors with which shop-

"You Irishmen woulda lost this war without allies like Texas and Russia."

owners shutter their establishments buckle and balloon out into grotesque swollen shapes.

Only once did a cartoon about civilians give the authorities gray hair and I didn't realize at the time that the drawing had anything to do with civilians. I merely wanted to give pictorial recognition to two of our most formidable allies—Texas and Ireland. The cartoon appeared in the Rome *Stars and Stripes,* a journal which enjoys a more high-brow audience than either the *New Yorker* or *Punch,* because it is the only daily paper available to the various embassies and legations in the city. But because it is published primarily for enlisted soldiers who are fighting a war, some of its contents cause these high brows to wrinkle in puzzled astonishment.

I was informed that the wife of the ambassador from Ireland to the Vatican had called the office and asked what gave in the cartoon department. She was told that no offense was meant and, when the cartoon was explained to her, she asked for copies she might send to Ireland, whose neutrality had not been violated, after all.

No button or shoelace escaped the eyes of the MPs and officers in Naples. I felt sorry for some of them, for I don't doubt that there were many who were nauseated by the job. Even if you had a pass, and it was typewritten properly (they hooked some combat men on this, because many company clerks tire of lugging typewriters around and fill in passes and reports with a pen), and you had your dogtags around your neck, you were not finished with the investigation.

If your pass showed you were a sergeant, and you didn't have your chevrons, they stuck you—ten dollars per stripe, or thirty for a buck sergeant. Now this was unfair as hell. If they wanted their rear men to wear stripes, that was okay. But an infantry noncom doesn't like to wear his stripes in battle because snipers pick on him. That selfish excuse didn't mean a thing to the in-

*"Straighten those shoulders! How long you been in
the army?"*

quisitors. He should carry a special set of chevrons, equipped
with zipper, for visits to Naples.

So it went. The doggie was snapped up the instant he stepped
off the boat coming back from Anzio. One soldier wrote *Stars
and Stripes* that he had been arrested and jailed for wearing his
combat infantry badge. The MPs didn't know what it was.

It was, not enough, the doggies felt, to live in unspeakable
misery and danger while these "gumshoe so-and-sos" worked in
the comfort and safety of the city. Hell, no. When they came
back to try to forget the war for a few days, these "rear echelon
goldbrickers" had to pester them to death.

When a man is feeling like this you can't tell him that his

"Th' hell with it, sir. Let's go back to the front."

tormentors are people like himself, and that they are in the rear because they have been ordered to work there, just as he was ordered to the front.

It wouldn't do any good to show him that these MPs and officers are a part of the tremendous machine that keeps him fed and clothed and supplied. It wouldn't do any good, because the doggie lives a primitive life and hasn't time for reasoning. He says to himself, "This is nothing but a bunch of rear echelon bastards," and goes back and tells his outfit about it. Soldiers who are in danger feel a natural and human resentment toward soldiers who aren't. You'll notice it every time you see men in muddy boots meet men wearing clean ties.

I drew many cartoons about it. I don't know how much trouble they caused the various editors of the paper but I do know that there was enough to go around.

One of the worst plagues for people who draw pictures in the army is the steady stream of requests to do free-lance art work. A cartoonist uses brush and ink; therefore he must also be adept at making signs with Old English letters, copying the Madonna and Child, and doing portraits ("Of course, I'll make it worth your while")—according to the minds of those who need signs, Madonnas, or portraits.

I can't letter worth a damn, I never tried a Madonna, and if I painted George Washington's portrait I'd probably make him look like Willie or Joe before I finished. So I've found a way to get around those people, and I'll pass it on to others who are in the same predicament.

I pass the request on to the editor, on the grounds that I can't sneeze, much less draw anything, without his orders. Since I keep the editor mystified about how much time I require to do six cartoons a week, he always refuses extracurricular requests because he's afraid I won't meet his deadlines. The more persistent folks who want me to do personal greeting cards and "Off Limits" signs for them have learned that my passing the buck to the editor amounts to a refusal, and soon they go and pick on somebody else whose editor isn't under any illusions about how long it takes to finish a routine drawing.

But once a request came when I was embroiled in the Battle of Naples, and since it came from a corps commander, I felt I couldn't afford to alienate any possible friends. The corps commander had set up an officers' club in an Italian yacht club. The windows were portholes and had to be blacked out with circular pieces of plywood at night.

The general's aide brought over two wooden disks on which the old man wanted pictures of Willie and Joe. I took a dim view of decorating officers' clubs, because I felt it would ruin my standing as an honorable enlisted man. But I worked out a satisfactory solution. I told the aide the drawings would be finished in a couple of days. It actually took fifteen minutes, but you can't afford to let people know you can work fast.

I painted Willie on one piece of plywood and Joe on the other. They looked like ordinary, life-size portraits until, the evening of the general's party, they were properly mounted in their circular holes.

Next morning, an officer secretly sympathetic with my cause reported that the party was not as lively as it might have been. Every time a beribboned staff officer with a highball in his hand lifted his eyes he found himself staring into the bearded face of a dirty, weary, disapproving dogface peering in the porthole with his fingertips on the sill.

People who make cartoons, according to legend, are supposed never to laugh. Perhaps I'm too young at the game to have the proper attitude, because I got a whale of a laugh out of another

"We oughta tell 'em th' whole army don't look like us, Joe."

incident that occurred in the midst of the Battle of Naples.

I made a drawing of Joe and Willie slouched in a ruined door-way and looking wearily at an admonishing rear echelon corporal.

Says Willie, "He's right, Joe. When we ain't fightin' we should ack like sojers."

The day after the cartoon was printed a pleasant old colonel

"He's right, Joe. When we ain't fightin' we should ack like sojers."

came into the *Stars and Stripes* office. He was quite evidently a new arrival, for he didn't know I was seditious. He hadn't bothered to study the drawing, which had taken a crack at the rigid regulations with regard to soldierly conduct behind the lines.

All the colonel knew was that when you weren't fighting you *were* supposed to have a military bearing. So he had a brilliant and highly original idea which he thought certain to win him a promotion or the Legion of Merit. He wanted, so help me, to take the original drawing and have thousands of huge poster copies printed. He planned to plaster them on every wall and telephone pole in Italy, as an admonition to GIs to "ack like sojers."

[83]

I was in a hell of a spot. He really looked like a nice guy, and I didn't want him slaughtered like a lamb, when he would probably start drawing retirement pay in a couple of years. But surely I couldn't say, "Sir, that's a treacherous cartoon, made to cause riots and rebellion among soldiers, and it would be a mistake to make posters of it and aid and abet my cause."

Instead, I gave him the drawing and, with brigadier's stars in his eyes, he headed for the door.

"The general will love this," he said.

I'm sure the general did.

Of all the world's armies, the American army gets the best equipment. The dogface knows that when he sees other armies. But we missed the boat on one thing. Every other army gets a liquor ration.

Drinking, like sex, is not a question of should or shouldn't in the army. It's here to stay, and it seems to us here that the best way to handle it is to understand and recognize it, and to arrange things so those who have appetites can satisfy them with a minimum of trouble for everybody. We have a pretty strong hunch that the army doesn't keep drinkin' likker out of our reach because the War Department is stupid. It's only because the home folks would scream their heads off at any hint of the clean-cut lads overseas besotting themselves. So stuff is bought at very high prices from street vendors over here. The dogfaces love to tell the story of the curious soldier who sent a bottle of cognac to a chemist friend for an analysis. In due time the report came back. It informed the soldier that his horse had kidney trouble. . . .

A liquor ration would seem to be a desirable thing. The British

EDITOR'S NOTE: Sergeant Mauldin has notified the publishers that shortly after he had written this section of the book the War Department granted officers (but not enlisted men) a liquor ration.

"It will comfort my ol' woman to know I have gave up rye whisky an' ten-cent seegars."

soldier gets a spot of whisky regularly, the size of the spot depending upon his rank. He gets a little beer also. And the Frenchman gets his wine. It's not much, but his palate is soothed with honest liquor which makes him unable to bear the smell, let

"Hell of a way to waste time. Does it work?"

alone the taste, of the home-distilled stuff the Americans are forced to drink because they can get nothing else.

The Arabs used to gather discarded British whisky bottles, fill them with unmentionable substances, and sell the hooch to the Americans for ten dollars a bottle.

Until some intelligent brass hat repaired a big brewery in Naples and started to send beer to Anzio, the boys at the beachhead were fixing up their own distilleries with barrels of dug-up vino, gasoline cans, and copper tubing from wrecked airplanes. The result was a fiery stuff which the Italians call grappa. The doggies called it "Kickapoo Joy Juice," and took the name from the popular "Li'l Abner" comic strip which *Stars and Stripes* printed daily. It wasn't bad stuff when you cut it with canned grapefruit juice.

"We're jest a coupla red-blooded American boys."

Troop commanders, who would seem to be the best judges of discipline and morale in their own outfits, usually looked the other way when they spotted one of these distilleries. Many troop commanders were, in fact, among the distilleries' best customers. I knew one CO who used to tip his boys off when members of the inspector general's office came around. He called them "revenooers."

These unauthorized gin mills, in spite of their crude apparatus, produced a drink much less corrosive than the bootleg stuff the Italian civilians offered. The local rotgut made many who drank it "crazy" drunk, not "respectable" drunk. That caused a few cases of ulcers, blindness, and God knows what.

Because drinking is a big thing in a dogface's life, I drew many pictures of guys wrapped around cognac bottles. I showed Willie and Joe, stewed to the ears, telling their captain, as an alibi, that they were "jest a coupla red-blooded American boys."

Too many sharp-eyed people noticed that there were three men in the picture, and *seven* hands; therefore, they were convinced that I was stewed to the ears myself and disqualified as a sober judge of the drinking problem.

Some guys brought the habit overseas with them, but I think the large majority drinks because other recreational facilities are crowded or unavailable, and liquor can dull the sharp memories of war.

That's something the American public just can't seem to realize, and that's why the European armies get good hooch and the Americans don't. The Europeans have seen war and armies at first hand. An army at war is far different from an army in its own homeland, and all soldiers' instincts are pretty much the same.

The Europeans know that soldiers are going to do some drinking, and, since they don't like to have their windows kicked in by joyful souses, they keep their soldiers' whistles wetted just enough to satisfy the boys, but not enough to souse them.

[88]

"Go tell th' boys to line up, Joe. We got fruit juice fer breakfast."

I'm not trying to say the American army is a drunken army. Most of the men have the same attitude as I have about liquor. I drink very little, and I don't like strong liquor at all. Yet there have been times over here when I have tied one on because I was homesick, or bored, or because I was sitting around with a bunch of guys who had a bottle, and when it came around to me I just

"Them rats! Them dirty, cold-blooded, sore-headed, stinkin' Huns! Them atrocity-committin' skunks . . ."

naturally took a belt at it. And there were many times that I guzzled wine because the water was questionable.

I don't think I'll carry a confirmed drinking habit back home with me. But until they send me home or send my wife over here, or until they ship over portable soda fountains, I'm going to do a little drinking now and then.

The Germans seemed to go out of their way to sabotage wineries. They were just like dogs; what they couldn't eat or drink or carry away, they messed up so nobody else could use it.

But they missed one opportunity. Corps headquarters in Anzio was set up in a twisting maze of catacombs far below the earth's

"Don't startle 'im, Joe. It's almost full."

surface. The tunnels had been used for wine storage for centuries, and once you got down there it was hard to leave. It wasn't only a good place to stay away from shells. Many of the little niches had big vino barrels.

Only once was the peace of the catacombs and the soft sound of gurgling vino disturbed. That was when a shell hit the officers' latrine on the surface and shattered the wooden stairs which led down into the caves. No officers were in the latrine when the shell struck, but the place was out of commission for some time, and when a high-ranking officer gets off his daily schedule it's a very unhappy day for his subordinates.

The Germans drank a lot of schnapps during that Anzio period. Among the first prisoners captured on the beachhead were several drunken German officers who had driven a volkswagen into the gaping doors of an LST. They must have had a terrible hangover when they woke up next morning.

I've used Willie and Joe in my cartoons because riflemen like them are the basic guys and the most important guys in a war. While there are many other weapons besides rifles even in a rifle company, and dozens of other branches which are a part of the general front, I haven't run into many objections because I stick to Willie and Joe and their rifles most of the time. Those who work nearest the front know that the rifleman has the hardest job. Occasionally, however, I have tried to branch out a little—with artillery and medics and engineers, mostly.

Germans respect our artillery, and I don't blame them. Our army seems less reluctant than the German army to expend shells instead of men. If one of our artillery observers in an infantry position sees a few Germans, he's very likely to get excited and throw a concentration of shells at them.

The battered krauts, who come from a land where shells are costly, lives are cheap, and logic governs action, can't understand why we didn't send an infantry patrol instead.

Nevertheless, their artillery is damned good—and in some

"Ordnance? Ah'm havin' trouble with mah shootin' arn."

(This cartoon was made on the Italian beachhead with inadequate equipment
and stamp-pad ink instead of drawing ink.)

places they have had us outgunned. Their 88mm. is the terror
of every dogface. It can do everything but throw shells around
corners, and sometimes we think it has even done that.

The infantryman hates shells more than anything else. He can

[9 3]

"I'll let ya know if I find th' one wot invented th' 88."

spend hours camouflaging himself against enemy observation, but the kraut who is twisting the controls on the 88 a couple of mountains away doesn't see what he is shooting at, and so his shell is just as likely to hit the good soldier who is under cover as the dumb one who is standing on top of a knoll.

The doggie becomes a specialist on shells after he has been

*"Ever notice th' funny sound these zippers make,
Willie?"*

in the line awhile. Sometimes he hates those that come straight
at him more than those that drop, because the high ones give
him more warning. On the other hand, if the flat one misses him
it keeps on traveling, while the dropped one can kill him even
if it misses him by dozens of yards. He has no love for either
kind.

Some shells scream, some whiz, some whistle and others whir.
Most flat-trajectory shells sound like rapidly ripped canvas.
Howitzer shells seem to have a two-toned whisper.

Let's get the hell off this subject.

Propaganda leaflets are used by both sides. Because we seem
to be winning the war, ours are generally more convincing, but

"Tell them leaflet people th' krauts ain't got time fer readin' today."

I think theirs sometimes show more ingenuity. They know our fondness for comic strips and often illustrate their leaflets. What these pamphlets lack in truth they make up in reader interest.

I remember one that arrived in Anzio one morning. It was so well-drawn and attractively colored that a lot of guys risked their necks to scramble out and get copies. It had something to do with a profiteer and an infantryman's wife in America. The continuity was awkward, but the pictures were spicy and the guys were hard up for reading matter.

Once a bunch of sadistic characters in a 105mm. howitzer outfit got a big batch of leaflet shells and didn't know what to do with them. Eventually they made up their minds. They knew that Jerry liked our leaflets. It was an American custom to shoot them over, give them time to scatter and fall to the ground, and then to cease all fire until the krauts could gather them. When they saw our propaganda coming, they would climb out of their cramped holes, light cigarettes, go to the toilet with the leaflets, or take a belt at the schnapps bottle. It was a pleasant five- or ten-minute break.

So the 105 battery crammed its guns full of propaganda and banged away until it was all used up. They waited just long enough for Jerry to get out of his hole and wrap himself around his bottle—then they piled in a concentration of high explosive.

Psychological Warfare probably got as sore about that as the surviving Germans. Our leaflet barrages were distrusted for a long, long time after that.

Mortars are the artillery of an infantry company. Outside of the bazooka, they carry more viciousness and wallop per pound than any weapon the infantry has. The guys who operate them are at a big disadvantage. Because of the mortar's limited range, they have to work so close to the front that they are a favorite target for snipers, patrols, shells, and countermortar fire. Knocked-out mortar positions earn Iron Crosses for ambitious young herrenvolk.

"K Comp'ny artillery commander speakin'."

The worst thing about mortars is that the Germans make them too. Their nastiest is the "screaming meemie." I never drew pictures about "screaming meemies" because they just aren't funny.

For a long time I loved to throw hooked cartoons at the Air Forces and other branches famed for their comfortable rear

*"You have completed your fiftieth combat patrol.
Congratulations. We'll put you on mortars awhile."*

echelon accommodations. One of the common gripes among the infantry is the way the fliers get to go home after some definite number of missions.

An Air Corps mission amounts to several hours of discomfort and considerable danger, after which the fliers return to their bases. Some of the airfields, particularly the fighter strips, are far from comfortable, but on the whole the flying boys do okay by themselves.

Recently I've changed some of my opinions. After a certain length of time overseas, you stop bitching at the guy who has something. You may wish you had it yourself, but you begin to realize that taking the warm coat off his back isn't going to

"Uncle Willie!"

make your back any warmer. So the more seasoned doggie just sort of wonders why he doesn't get to go home after a certain number of "missions." He laughs about the youthfulness of the Air Corps officers and he wishes somebody looked after him as well as somebody looks after the Air Corps. But he doesn't bitch when he sees a formation of planes going through heavy flak and he feels pretty awful when he sees one go down and thinks of the guys in it.

As the war goes on, a sort of undeclared fraternity develops. It might be called "The Benevolent and Protective Brotherhood of Them What Has Been Shot At." So, while the infantryman may go on griping because *he* doesn't get 50 per cent extra pay for dangerous duty, and because *he* can't go back to a base when

"Hullo, glamorous."
"Howdy, blitzkrieg."

his mission is accomplished, when he talks to a man who is flak-happy from too many hours in the substratosphere buzzing with enemy fighters he has a tendency to sympathize with the airman, even when the doggie himself is battle-happy.

It would be pretty hard to define an infantry "mission." It

". . . forever, Amen. Hit the dirt."

goes on twenty-four hours a day, seven days a week, and the infantryman has everything from planes and tanks to grenades and bullets thrown at him, to say nothing of flame throwers, mines, booby traps, and shells. When he has had a year or two of this he has, in the opinion of many of us, completed enough missions to merit him a hundred "rest cures." He is damned lucky if he gets a three-day pass to a town swarming with other soldiers.

Once I watched a tank battle from as great a distance as I could keep without sacrificing visibility. I wasn't anxious to get any closer because the American tanks were tangling with some very efficient Panzers.

I tried to draw a picture of the battle itself, but no cartoon could have mirrored that scene. The only drawing that came out of the immense spectacle of crawling, turning, spitting, dying monsters was one about the pooped-out crews who crawled out of the tanks for a breath of air before they rumbled back into battle.

Religious services in battle zones offer weird contrast to bursting shells and the twisted wreckage of war. It is strange to see reverence helmeted and armored.

I saw a Catholic chaplain at Salerno gather up his white robes and beat a Focke-Wulf's tracers into a muddy ditch by a split second, then return and carry on the service as if nothing had happened. I have a lot of respect for those chaplains who keep up the spirits of the combat guys. They often give the troops a pretty firm anchor to hang onto.

For some time I experienced a recurring battle between my cartoon deadlines and my sense of respect for the holy. I let the former win in one cartoon, but since then my righteous side has ignored the deadlines.

Once a British friend on the Eighth Army paper asked me why I didn't draw something about them. So I did.

"You blokes leave an awfully messy battlefield."

There was a standing joke for a while between the British division at Anzio and one of the American divisions. The Americans, noted for their wealth of matériel, often littered the area with discarded equipment, and the thrifty British who relieved them just couldn't understand it. If a British colonel draws an unnecessary pair of shoes for his regimental supply, he's likely to get a court-martial out of it, and God help the Tommy who loses his Enfield rifle.

So the British used to accuse the Americans of leaving a messy battlefield, and I drew a picture of a Tommy telling that to two dogfaces. The British up there seemed to like it okay, and the doggies at Anzio caught it. But the British brass in Naples made a complaint. They didn't understand the picture, but they were certain it was anti-British.

I was sorry that happened, because I think the offended ones belonged to a minority, and the British would have given me quite a lot of opportunities for cartooning.

Their drivers are a little trouble sometimes, because they can't get used to the right-hand side of the highways, and they are often cussed at by our guys. Their brass hats are very stuffy, like a lot of ours, and I think it would have been a pleasure to work on them.

If you can get behind an Englishman's unholy fear of making a friend until he has known the candidate for at least five years, you will find him a pretty good egg. I made a drawing for private circulation among the staff of *Union Jack,* the British army paper, and I had a gratifying feeling that they understood the American sense of humor. The drawing was one of the commanding officer of *Union Jack.*

Chemical Warfare is a big branch which has seldom been noticed because the Germans haven't yet started to gas us. The CWs must have some high-pressure dime-store salesmen working in their midst, judging by the screwy little gadgets with which they love to load the infantry. Still, their 4.2 chemical mortars

[105]

"I see Comp'ny E got th' new-style gas masks."

have done a tremendous and unrecognized job of blasting the
pants off the krauts with high explosive and phosphorus.

Once in a while I've been guilty of drawing certain pictures
to get a grudge out of my system. One time when I was driving
my jeep I got caught in a convoy of quartermaster trucks and

"You'd hurry home too if you lived in a ration dump!"

I became very unhappy as the miles rolled by. It was the worst convoy I had ever seen. If one driver got tired of looking at the rear of the preceding truck, he would, without any signal, pull around the offending vehicle and pass it so he could gaze at the rear of the next truck. The whole column was clipping along at sixty miles an hour, hogging the road, and making things very unpleasant indeed for everybody else on the road. I was knocked into the ditch twice.

That made me draw my first Quartermaster cartoon. A little while later the French army started tearing up the roads, and they made our worst quartermaster drivers seem like timid old ladies. All a Frenchman knows about a truck is the general loca-

*"Some of you may not come back. A French convoy has been
reported on the road."*

tion of the foot throttle. French convoys stop simply by smashing into one another's bumpers.

I made a complete turnabout and did a cartoon favoring the quartermasters vs. the French. I was merely working off steam

"I'll be darned! Here's one wot wuz wrecked in combat."

and I doubt very much if I influenced or was even noticed by the quartermasters or the French, who were too busy denting each other's fenders. There was a slight stink about the French drawing, because some authorities were afraid our allies might not take that kind of ribbing. Apparently they did.

I got downright affectionate toward the quartermasters in France, where they did a miraculous job of supplying the combat troops. The gasoline problem was fierce, because the combat men had moved so far ahead of the supply schedule, but the QMs delivered the goods.

Army supply is a tremendous machine which works efficiently and quietly—so quietly that it is hardly noticed by the combat

"I calls her Florence Nightingale."

troops, who never wonder where their stuff is coming from and don't hesitate to yell when it fails to arrive.

But I was getting too soft, and so I had to throw one at the quartermasters and the French and everybody else except Ord-

"Best little mine detector made."

nance. The ordnance men were too busy patching up the vehicles these gasoline cowboys had wrecked.

I'm sure I didn't hurt any feelings, for nobody paid any attention to me while I was flailing around with my brush and ink bottle. They had more important things to do.

When the mountain fighting in Italy first started to get tough, and it was impossible for trucks or jeeps to bring food, water, and ammo up the mountain trails, mule companies were mustered and calls for experienced mule skinners went out through the divisions. Mules were sought out and bought from farmers. They carried supplies to many soldiers who hadn't seen a jeep for weeks. Many of them were undoubtedly blood relatives of the

"Damn fine road, men!"

beloved Maggie of World War I who had been left overseas
after she kicked hell out of her regimental commander to the
delight of one and all.

It would have gladdened the hearts of those old soldiers at
home, who were convinced that this new army was going crazy

"Yer lucky. Yer learnin' a trade."

with newfangled inventions, to see long columns of balky mules being cajoled and threatened up the trails by their bearded, swearing, sweating skinners.

Once I thought I did a very funny cartoon. It was a picture of an old-time cavalryman shooting his jeep, which had a broken axle. It is one of those cartoon ideas you think up rarely; it has simplicity, it tells a story, it doesn't need words. It is, I believe, the very best kind of cartoon.

At the time I was stationed at Fort Devens with my division, the feature editor of *Yank,* the army weekly, asked me to send him some stuff. I did, but he didn't like the material. He had just come from a civilian magazine, where the only army car-

toons showed jeeps jumping over mountains. After about a dozen drawings, I stopped sending stuff to him, but he did use the cavalry cartoon. He reduced it to postage-stamp size and ran it on the last column of the last page. One sneeze by the puniest typesetter and I'd have been blown right off the page. Since that time I have found those *Yank* employees whom I have met to be pleasant people, but I have never quite forgiven that feature editor.

I revived the old cavalry sergeant in the *Stars and Stripes,* where I have a regular two-column space which can't be made any smaller. I shall keep reviving that cartoon until somebody appreciates it.

If I were trying to tell somebody about the war, I would certainly say more about the engineers. But I don't know how

"Don't hurry for me, son. I like to see young men take an interest in their work."

they bolt braces on Bailey bridges, and I don't know the finer points of neutralizing a Teller mine, so I can't draw many pictures about them, except as they come into contact with the infantry.

"This is Fragrant Flower Advance. Gimme yer goddam number."

Combat engineers carry rifles and often use them. When they put down their rifles they have to pick up their tools.

I intended the picture of the professional fighting man and the man who is laboring on a road as pure sarcasm. The cartoon was probably understood by few people outside the engineers and infantry. The fighting man won't be able to put his knowledge to good use after the war, and the muddy engineer probably owned a fleet of trucks in civil life.

Mine detectors are always good cartoon material, but unfortunately you can't draw very realistic cartoons about them, because mine detectors are seldom used for anything but detecting mines. That's the trouble with drawing pictures about specialists and their equipment. All these guys are fighting a war, and some of the time they are doing it in great danger. They develop a rather serious turn of mind, and so an engineer might stare with some wonderment if you tried to show his life with his mine detector in a series of gags. He's usually a little scared when he's poking around in a minefield, and he stopped feeling silly about it a long time ago.

The guy who thinks up names for Liberty ships has a relative over here. The relative thinks up names for telephone codes.

Instead of saying, "This is Company A; give me G-3 at Division CP, advance," he says, "Able Jackson company calling Jehoshaphat 3." That's to confuse any wire tappers from the Third Reich who might be listening.

You can take the cartoon and go on from there.

The medics are good subjects for drawings, and anybody who does stuff about the infantry has to throw in the medics once in a while. They are a lot like the other branches. The farther you work toward the front, the simpler and rougher life gets, and a few more human and good things show up.

The aid man is the dogface's family doctor, and he is regarded as an authority on every minor ailment from a blister to a cold

"It's okay, Joe. I'm a noncombatant."

in the head. The aid man usually takes this responsibility quite seriously. He lances and patches blisters with all the professional pride of a brain specialist removing a tumor. He watches over his boys and sees that their water is pure or, if there is no water, he looks at the wine barrel.

But the dogface's real hero is the litter bearer and aid man who goes into all combat situations right along with the infantryman, shares his hardships and dangers, and isn't able to fight back. When the infantryman is down, the medic must get up and help him. That's not pleasant sometimes when there's shooting.

The aid men and litter bearers know that their work is often far more important than that of the surgeon at the operating

"Hell. Just when I git me practice built up they transfer me to another regiment."

table; because if it were not for the aid man the casualty would not live to reach the surgeon's table.

Let's say the doggie has a shattered leg and is lying in a shell hole out in front of his company, which is pinned down by machine-gun fire. He uses the bandage from his first-aid packet

"I'm jest a country doctor. If ya don't mind, I'll consult wit'
Pfc. Johnson, th' famous blister specialist."

to make a tourniquet, and he takes the sulfa pills, but he knows
that if he lies there much longer he will bleed to death.

Nobody is going to blame the aid man if he saves his own neck
and doesn't go out after a man who will probably die anyway.
But the medic usually goes. If the Germans are feeling pretty

"Quit beefin' or I'll send ya back to th' infantry."

good, they might lift their fire when they see his red-cross armband.

Put yourself in the wounded guy's shoes when he sees the medic appear over him, and his pain is dulled by morphine, his bleeding is stopped, and he is lifted out and carried back to safety and good surgery. Sure, he's going to love that medic. And after a few dozen men owe their lives to one man, that little pill roller is going to be very well liked indeed.

Sooner or later, like everybody who works around the infantry, the medic is going to get his. Many aid men have been wounded and many have been killed. It should comfort the families of those who have died to know that there are many friends who grieve with them.

"I think he should at least try to lie at attention."

But if I say much more than this the commissioned intern who entered my ward in Naples one winter when I was recovering from pneumonia and ordered me to lie at attention, if I couldn't sit or stand at attention when I saw him coming, will show this around and say:

"See? I told you we medics did a great job!"

It's a hell of a thing that some brass hats have made front-line medics turn in their combat badges. If the brass did it because the medic doesn't fight, and the enemy might take the badge the wrong way if they capture him, that's reasonable. But they should have given him something to replace it—maybe a cross instead of a rifle on the badge.

[122]

EDITOR'S NOTE: The War Department recently restored combat badges to the front-line medics.

"Ya don't git combat pay 'cause ya don't fight."

I say that because it's important. Everybody these days wears combat boots and combat jackets. A lot of people who never saw more infantry than basic training wear the infantry blue on their caps. The combat badge is about the only thing that sets the front-line man apart, and he has reason to be proud of it.

"Who started th' rumor I wuz playin' poker wit' a beautiful nurse?"

When they took the badges away, the infantry howled louder than the medics. I'm convinced that the combat badge means much more to the front-line soldier than the small amount of extra pay that goes with it. It is a symbol of what he has been through. Many troops who operate with the infantry should get it and don't and a few who shouldn't get it do.

I was hanging around a regiment in a rest area near Nancy, in France, when a group of doggies brought the subject up. A medic was in the group. He had plenty of guys speaking for him so he didn't say anything.

"Who's the stupid bastard what did it?"

"What the hell they think they're doing?"

"Our regimental clerks are wearing big combat badges and they take it away from one of our medics two days before a blurp gun cuts him in two!"

"Hell of a goddam note!"

But the direst threat of all came from a little Browning Automatic rifleman with thick glasses:

"Wait'll Ernie Pyle hears about this!"

When a soldier gets out of an army hospital he will most likely be thrown into a "repple depple." This institution, identified in army regulations as a replacement depot, is a sort of clearinghouse through which soldiers who have been separated from their outfits or soldiers newly arrived from the States have to pass for reassignment.

I went through a repple depple at Palermo, Sicily, and my experience seems to have been typical. This establishment was operated by a paratrooper lieutenant (I don't know why, either) who spent most of his time convincing us that paratrooping had a great postwar future. Several times I interrupted him to say that my outfit was only fifteen miles away and couldn't I get over to them. Each time he told me that a truck would come within a few hours and pick me up. I believed this until I discov-

"I guess it's okay. The replacement center says he comes from a long line of infantrymen."

ered two other guys from my outfit who had been waiting for this same truck for three weeks.

I guess the repple depple people didn't trust us, because the place was surrounded by a very high wall and there were guards beyond that.

We waited until night fell, then we plotted our "break." We persuaded one inmate, whose outfit had already gone and who had given up hope of salvation, to distract the guard while we went over the wall. As far as I know they still have my name and I'm still AWOL from a repple depple. I joined my outfit and caught the last boat to Salerno.

Later I learned that soldiers often languish in repple depples for months, only to be snapped up eventually by some outfit with

"I got a nasty letter from your poor wife, Joe. You better give her an allotment after I pay you back that loan."

which they are not familiar. A soldier's own outfit is the closest thing to home he has over here, and it is too bad when he has to change unnecessarily.

I heard of a soldier who spent his entire time overseas in repple depples, and went home on rotation without ever having been assigned. His home-town paper called him "a veteran of the Italian campaign."

The attitude of the dogface toward America and the home front is a complex thing. Nobody loves his own land more than a soldier overseas, and nobody swears at it more. He loves it because he appreciates it after seeing the horrible mess that has been made of Europe.

He has seen unbelievable degeneracy and filth in Mediterranean towns where mothers sell their daughters and daughters sell their mothers and little kids sell their sisters and themselves. He has seen the results of the German occupation of France and the fury of the French people and their savage revenge upon anything German. He has seen stark fear and utter destruction and horrible hunger. But at the same time he has seen families bravely trying to rebuild their shattered homes, and he has seen husbands and wives with rifles fighting ahead of him in France. He knows how they can throw themselves completely and unselfishly into the war when it is necessary.

So he is naturally going to get sore when he thinks of selfishness at home. He got just as sore at the big company which was caught bribing inspectors and sending him faulty armor for his tanks as he did at the workers who held up production in vital factories. He doesn't have time to go into economics and labor-management problems. All he knows is that he is expected to make great sacrifices for little compensation, and he must make those sacrifices whether he likes it or not. Don't expect him to weigh the complicated problem before he gets sore. He knows he delivered and somebody else didn't.

But, in spite of these irritations, the soldier's pride in his country is immense. He's proud of the splendid equipment he gets from home, and sometimes he even gets a little overbearing about it.

Often soldiers who are going home say they are going to tell the people how fortunate we were to stop the enemy before he

"I tried one of them labor-management argyments wit' Looten-ant Atkins."

was able to come and tear up our country. They are also going to tell the people that it is a pretty rough life over here.

I've tried to do that in my drawings and I know that many thousands of guys who have gone back have tried to do it, too. But no matter how much we try we can never give the folks at

*"Congratulations. You're the 100th soldier who has
posed with that bottle of Icey Cola. You may drink it."*

home any idea of what war really is. I guess you have to go
through it to understand its horror. You can't understand it by
reading magazines or newspapers or by looking at pictures or
by going to newsreels. You have to smell it and feel it all around
you until you can't imagine what it used to be like when you
walked on a sidewalk or tossed clubs up into horse chestnut trees
or fished for perch or when you did anything at all without a
pack, a rifle, and a bunch of grenades.

We all used to get sore at some of the ads we saw in magazines
from America. The admen should have been required by law to
submit all copy to an overseas veteran before they sent it to the
printers.

*"Don't mention it, lootenant. They mighta replaced
ya wit' one of them salutin' demons."*

I remember one lulu of a refrigerator ad showing a lovely,
dreamy-eyed wife gazing across the blue seas and reflecting on
how much she misses Jack . . . BUT she knows he'll never be
content to come back to his cozy nest (equipped with a Frosty
refrigerator; sorry, we're engaged in vital war production now)
until the Hun is whipped and the world is clean for Jack's little
son to grow up in.

Chances are that Jack, after eighteen or twenty months of
combat, is rolling his eyes and making gurgling sounds every
time the company commander comes around, so the old man
will think he is battle-happy and send him home on rotation. Like
hell Jack doesn't want to come home now.

And when he does come home you can bet he'll buy some other

brand of refrigerator with his demobilization pay, just to spite the Frosty adman.

When Bing Crosby returned to America after his visit to the French front, he told reporters, according to one news dispatch, that entertainment is needed most by the dispirited troops of the rear echelon rather than by the front-line soldiers. Up there, it seemed to him, "morale is sky-high, clothes are cleaner and salutes really snap." The dogfaces who read that dispatch in the foxholes didn't know what front Bing was talking about.

Please, God, don't let anybody become a lecturer on front-line conditions until he has spent at least a year talking to the combat men. Many of us over here have been trying to find out about the front for several years and we feel like anything but experts.

One thing that caused a lot of howls among the soldiers was the way celebrities, particularly female ones, were always surrounded by officers.

Some celebrities couldn't help this, some encouraged it, and others just didn't know any better. Most of the blame should go to the officers. It was pretty awful to see a string of them tagging behind some little Hollywood chick. Several memorable ladies of the screen actually managed to break away from the howling pack and escape to the enlisted men, but there were very few such escapes.

I know officers like to see women from home as much as anybody else does, but I think the enlisted men should have been given a chance to see the girls.

Officers around the front were good Joes about it. The success of their jobs depended upon the morale of their men, and very

[132]

"Just gimme a coupla aspirin. I already got a Purple Heart."

few combat COs tried to horn in on the dogfaces' entertainment.

Decorations are touchy things to talk about. The British kid us because we're overdecorated, and perhaps we are in some ways.

Civilians may think it's a little juvenile to worry about ribbons,

"Eeeeeek!"

but a civilian has a house and a bankroll to show what he's done for the past few years.

I thought the War Department ruined any value the Good Conduct ribbon may have had by passing it out to men who had only one year of service. But it's different with those medals which are given only for heroism in battle. You can bet that any man decorated for heroism has earned the award, because the committee that gave him the decoration first called in a hell of a lot of witnesses.

I have four ribbons, and I haven't had so many troubles as a lot of men who finished the last war with a single campaign ribbon. But sometimes I'm a little proud of those four ribbons, and I often put them on under my sweater and peek at them when nobody is looking.

To the dogface out on patrol, his platoon command post, with its machine-gun emplacement, is rear echelon and home and the safest place in the world.

The gunner in the platoon CP is itching to get the hell out of there and back to the safety of company headquarters, where the topkick is equally anxious to find an excuse to visit Battalion.

The radio operators in Battalion like to go after extra tubes at Regimental supply, even though Regimental seldom stocks tubes, and the guys who work at field desks in Regimental hate the guts of those rear echelon bastards in Division. Division feels that way about Corps, Corps about Army, Army about Base Section, and, so help me Hannah, Base Section feels that way about soldiers in the States.

Months after the new combat boots and jackets arrived in Italy many front-line soldiers still wore soaked leggings and flimsy field jackets. The new clothing was being shortstopped by some of the rear echelon soldiers who wanted to look like the combat men they saw in the magazines. None of these shortstoppers took the clothing with any direct intention of denying the stuff to guys at the front. I suppose these fellows in the rear

"Wot do ya mean, 'It's nice to git back to th' rear echelon'? Ya been out huntin' souvenirs agin?"

just looked at the mountainous heap of warm combat jackets piled in a supply dump and didn't see anything wrong with swiping a couple for themselves. After several hundred thousand men had grabbed at the heap there weren't many new boots and jackets left.

*"Git his pistol, Joe. I know where we kin swap it fer
a combat jacket an' some boots."*

The army had shipped over only enough of the new clothing
to supply the men in the foxholes, and because of this rear echelon pilfering, thousands of dogfaces at the front shivered in the
mud and the rain while guys at the rear wore the combat clothes
in warm offices.

You can see that it was a big gripe, and a justifiable one. If a
soldier appeared in combat togs behind the battle zone, he was
often stopped by a doggie and asked what he did for a living
in the armed service of his country. If his answer was unsuitable,
he was shoved into some alley whence he would emerge wearing
the thin field jacket and wet leggings of his still outraged but
now better dressed challenger.

The cartoon in which Willie tells Joe to grab the kraut's pistol and swap it for combat clothes probably didn't mean much to troops outside the Mediterranean theater. But in Italy those who understood it best were, strangely, those conscientious souls in the rear who stubbornly insisted that combat suits were for combat men, and not for the guy who pounded a typewriter at Army Headquarters and particularly not for the officer who supervised the pounding.

During the winter I acquired a pair of parachutists' jump boots—the most comfortable, well-built footwear issued by the army. They were a present from some guys in the 509th Parachute Battalion and, although I was deeply grateful, I always had a twinge when I wore the boots in town. I felt that a barefoot paratrooper shivered in every alley and followed me wherever I went.

There is a class of soldiers, midway between the front and rear—"too far forward to wear ties an' too far back to git shot." In this group there were a few men whose conduct, unfortunately, was taken by many combat men as typical of the entire class. I called these few men "garritroopers," to the subsequent protest of some paratroopers who felt that I had intended a crack at them. I really had not.

The garritroopers are able to look like combat men or like the rear soldiers, depending upon the current fashion trend. When the infantry was unpublicized and the Air Forces were receiving much attention, the emphasis was on beauty, and in every Army headquarters and midway supply dump you could shave yourselves with the garritrooper's trouser creases and use his shoes for a mirror. He would not wear ordinary GI trousers and shoes,

[138]

"We calls 'em garritroopers. They're too far forward to wear ties an' too far back to git shot."

but went in for sun glasses, civilian oxfords, and officers' forest-green clothing.

This burned up many decidedly unglamorous airplane mechanics who worked for a living and didn't look at all like the Air Force men the garritrooper saw in the magazines. It also

burned many honest GIs, who automatically saluted the garritrooper before they noticed that his officer's shirt had no insignia
on the collar.

It's true that many of the worst and most confirmed garritroopers were officers, who also affected the dark glasses and
crushed caps of the birdmen, but much as he winced, the combat
man didn't complain about them.

Some months later the infantry began to get attention. It took
the doughfoots a long time to become accustomed to the new
combat badges and extra pay. They were like ragged little step-
children who had found a winning lottery ticket.

It didn't take the garritroopers long to switch clothes. They
climbed out of the glamor rags and tossed the twenty-dollar
sun glasses into the gutter. "Be dirty, be rough, be scuffed," they
shouted. If they rode to town on a truck, they hung their faces
over the side to get a coat of dust. They let their whiskers grow.
They ripped holes in their pants and pounded their shoes with
rocks. You could get five fancy officers' shirts for one tattered
combat jacket, and if that jacket had a gen-yu-wine bullet hole
you could name your own price.

Bands of the garritroopers would hound a poor khaki-clad
clerk, on his way home after a hard day at the office. They would
yell, "Haw! Goddam base section. Rear echelon goldbrick."
And the base section clerk had to take it, because in his section
regulations about clothing were quite strictly enforced.

The average doggie, sick of dirt, will make some effort to clean
up when he gets one of those rare opportunities to go back to a
city and he certainly doesn't want to start any fighting when he
gets there.

[1 4 0]

"That can't be no combat man. He's lookin' fer a fight."

So he is rather surprised when he enters a town he remembers having taken last month, and finds it full of rough, bearded wild men, who seem to be in the process of taking it again, for they are yelling like hell, smashing windows and tossing empty vino bottles at "those damned rear echelon goldbricks."

"Let 'im in. I wanna see a critter I kin feel sorry fer."

Every now and then the garritroopers would mistake a freshly scrubbed infantryman for a rear man. When this happened the doggie was usually too disgusted to protest.

But the saddest thing about the whole business was that a surprisingly large number of those khaki-clad little men far behind

"Maybe Joe needs a rest. He's talkin' in his sleep."

the battle, the men resented by doggie and cursed by garritrooper, had seen months of combat before being put on limited service because of wounds or exhaustion.

Dig a hole in your back yard while it is raining. Sit in the hole until the water climbs up around your ankles. Pour cold mud down your shirt collar. Sit there for forty-eight hours, and, so there is no danger of your dozing off, imagine that a guy is sneaking around waiting for a chance to club you on the head or set your house on fire.

Get out of the hole, fill a suitcase full of rocks, pick it up, put a shotgun in your other hand, and walk on the muddiest road you can find. Fall flat on your face every few minutes as you imagine big meteors streaking down to sock you.

After ten or twelve miles (remember—you are still carrying the shotgun and suitcase) start sneaking through the wet brush. Imagine that somebody has booby-trapped your route with rattlesnakes which will bite you if you step on them. Give some friend a rifle and have him blast in your direction once in a while.

Snoop around until you find a bull. Try to figure out a way to sneak around him without letting him see you. When he does see you, run like hell all the way back to your hole in the back yard, drop the suitcase and shotgun, and get in.

If you repeat this performance every three days for several months you may begin to understand why an infantryman sometimes gets out of breath. But you still won't understand how he feels when things get tough.

One thing is pretty certain if you are in the infantry—you aren't going to be very warm and dry while you sleep. If you haven't thrown away your blankets and shelter half during a march, maybe you can find another guy who has kept his shelter half and the two of you can pitch a pup tent. But pup tents aren't very common around the front. Neither is sleep, for that matter. You do most of your sleeping while you march. It's not a very healthy sleep; you might call it a sort of coma. You can't

"A experienced field sojer will figure out a way to sleep warm an' dry. Lemme know when ya do."

hear anybody telling you to move faster but you can hear a whispering whoosh when the enemy up ahead stops long enough to throw a shell at you.

You don't feel very good when you wake up, because there is a thick fuzz in your head and a horrible taste in your mouth

"Ya wouldn't git so tired if ya didn't carry extra stuff. Throw th' joker outta yer decka cards."

and you wish you had taken your toothbrush out before you threw your pack away.

It's a little better when you can lie down, even in the mud. Rocks are better than mud because you can curl yourself around the big rocks, even if you wake up with sore bruises where the little rocks dug into you. When you wake up in the mud your cigarettes are all wet and you have an ache in your joints and a rattle in your chest.

You get back on your feet and bum a cigarette from somebody who had sense enough to keep a pack dry inside the webbing of his helmet liner. The smoke makes the roof of your mouth taste worse but it also makes you forget the big blister on your right heel. Your mind is still foggy as you finger the stubble on your face and wonder why there are no "Burma Shave" signs along the road so you could have fun reading the limericks and maybe even imagine you're walking home after a day's work.

Then you pick up your rifle and your pack and the entrenching tool and the canteen and the bayonet and the first-aid kit and the grenade pouches. You hang the bandoleer around your neck and you take the grenades out of the pouches and hang them on your belt by the handles.

You look everything over and try to find something else you can throw away to make the load on the blister a little lighter. You chuckle as you remember the ad you saw in the tattered magazine showing the infantryman going into battle with a gas mask and full field pack.

Then you discover something and you wonder why the hell you didn't think of it long ago—the M-1 clip pouches on your cartridge belt are just the right size for a package of cigarettes. That will keep the rain off the smokes.

You start walking again but you are getting close now so you keep five yards between yourself and the next guy and you begin to feel your heart pounding a little faster. It isn't so bad when you get there—you don't have time to get scared. But it's bad going there and coming back. Going there you think of what

"This damn tree leaks."

might happen and coming back you remember what did happen and neither is pleasant to think about.

Of course, nothing's really going to get you. You've got too much to live for. But you might get hurt and that would be bad. You don't want to come back all banged up. Why the hell doesn't

"Me future is settled, Willie. I'm gonna be a expert on types of European soil."

somebody come up and replace you before you get hurt? You've been lucky so far but it can't last forever.

You feel tighter inside. You're getting closer. Somebody said that fear is nature's protection for you and that when you get scared your glands make you more alert. The hell with nature.

"Now that ya mention it, Joe, it does sound like th'
patter of rain on a tin roof."

You'd rather be calm the way everybody else seems to be. But you know they're just as jumpy as you are.

Now they're pulling off the road. Maybe you don't have to go up there tonight. You don't. You start to dig a slit trench because the enemy might come to you if you don't go to him. But there's a big root halfway down. Mud and roots seem to follow you wherever you go. You dig around the root and then you try the hole for size. You look at the sky and it looks like rain.

A weapons carrier slithers up the trail and the driver tosses out the packs you all threw away a couple of miles back. Maybe the army is getting sensible. Hell, you got the wrong pack and somebody else got yours. The blankets are damp but they would have been soaked anyway even if you had carried them.

You throw some brush in the bottom of the trench. You squeeze in. You don't like it. You get out and sleep beside the hole. You wake up two hours later and you're glad you didn't get in the hole because it's raining and the hole is half full of water. Your head still feels fuzzy and your heart is still pounding but it's better because you have been lying down. A pool of water has collected right in the center of the shelter half you threw over yourself and the water is dribbling right through to your skin. You brush the water out and pull the canvas tight around you. The rain continues, the weather is getting colder, and you try to go to sleep quick so you won't feel it.

Sometimes when the doggies are on the march they find a gutted house with part of the roof still hanging out from the top of the wall. This makes very fine shelter indeed and it's a happy time when they go into bivouac near such a house. But when the guys are really lucky they find a barn, and every doggie knows that barns are far better than houses. He knows that vermin are awful things to have and, since he never gets a chance to take a bath, he avoids houses and questionable mattresses if he can find a luxurious barn full of hay. A farmer who has reason to be suspicious of soldiers prefers to have the guys sleep in his barns because even if the doggies swipe some hay they can't carry off his favorite rocking chair and daughter.

When you are in a barn you don't have to bother about being nice to the hostess because she is probably a cow. You can put one blanket under you and one over you and lots of hay on top of that and you will be very, very warm.

*"Aim between th' eyes, Joe. Sometimes they charge when they're
wounded."*

The only bad thing about a barn is that you find a lot of rats
there. You don't mind it so much when they just scurry over you
if they leave your face alone and don't get curious about your
anatomy. A barn rat likes nothing better than to bed down with
his guest and carry on a conversation in Braille all night.

Breakfast in bed.

The best nights I've spent in the field have been in barns. And the best night I ever spent in a barn was when I woke up and found a cow standing over me. She had a calf but I shouldered the little creature aside and milked the mother in my best New Mexico style. The farmer came in when I was almost finished

"We gotta probe fer Willie."

and I pointed to a small lump on the cow's udder. That showed
he hadn't stripped her well and I showed him how to do a nice
job of stripping with thumb and forefinger. He was well
content when I left and so was I because that was the first fresh
milk I had drunk since I left the States.

The dogfaces love to find haystacks and an infantry company will tear down a stack in five minutes. They line their holes with the stuff and, if they've got bedsacks, they'll fill them too. If they don't have bedsacks they find some stack that hasn't been torn down and dozens of guys will crawl into this one stack and disappear. It's wonderfully soft and wonderfully warm but if it's old hay a lot of people who suffer from hay fever have to pass it up. But even if you don't have hay fever there's another bad thing about haystacks: the enemy has used them and he figures you are going to use them too, so he often mines them and, if he is within shooting range, every now and then throws a shell into them. Bombers and artillerymen blow up haystacks and barns just on general principle sometimes.

Caves are nice and you find them sometimes in the mountains. Nice thing about a cave is that you can throw up a little dirt around the entrance and you're safe from almost anything. Air bursts and butterfly bombs make open holes uncomfortable sometimes.

Barns are still about the best, though.

Abandoned towns are wonderful places for guys who have time to make homes in them. Many doggies prefer wrecked houses to undamaged houses because as long as there are walls to break the wind and a roof to stop the weather the men can fix the places up without any qualms about scrounging.

There is a difference between scrounging and looting. Looting is the stealing of valuables, but most evacuees take their valuables with them. Scrounging is the borrowing of things which will make life in the field a little more bearable. Since the infantryman carries everything on his back, he can scrounge only

"Who is it?"

temporarily, borrowing a chair from this house and bedsprings from that one.

The headquarters units which follow the infantry have a little motor transport and they can carry many things with them. Go into almost any field CP and you'll find a pale-pink upholstered chair which looks pretty silly sitting there in the mud.

In combat, infantry officers usually share the same conditions as the dogfaces. But when the doggies get back to a temporary rest area they have to be careful about fixing up a wrecked house too well because the officers may suddenly remember that they are officers and take over the premises. Noncoms can be just as bad about it, too.

It's strange how memories of peacetime life influence these

"Don't tell 'em now, lieutenant. Wait'll they fix th' stove."

makeshift homes. If a soldier has fixed himself a dugout or an abandoned house, and has cleaned it up and made it look presentable, his visitors instinctively feel that this is a man's house, and he is its head. They use his C-ration can ash trays and they don't spit on the floor. But no matter how much time or effort a guy

*"Take off yer hat when ya mention sex here. It's a
reverint subject."*

is able to spend making his dugout livable, and no matter how
many of his friends may come to shoot the breeze with him, there
are only a few subjects of conversation: wives and girls and
families, just plain women, or home.

Many dugouts in Anzio were fixed up surprisingly well. Some
guys sat there for five months without moving, and they had to
do something to relieve their boredom. They scrounged a little
lumber here, a set of bedsprings there, and some of the boys even
found mirrors.

The farther behind the front line the dugouts were made the
more elaborate they became. Some blossomed out with reading
lamps made from salvaged jeep headlights and batteries, and a
few huts had wooden floors and real rugs and charcoal stoves

"Fire two more fer effect, Joe. I'm makin' a stovepipe."

made from German gas cans and the flexible tubing that had
been used to waterproof vehicles for the landing. Old brass from
shells made good stove parts, and the thick cardboard shell cases
were used to line walls and to make "sidewalks" through the
mud.

All the dugouts were sunk deep in the sandy, damp ground,

and had thick roofs made of layers of logs and planks and dirt. That made them almost invulnerable to shells. Guys who were able to find enough planks to line their walls combined insulation and decoration by covering them with cardboard wallpaper from ration boxes. But these more elaborate jobs weren't to be found very often right up at the front, because the guys up there couldn't move around freely enough to do any scrounging.

The Germans must be given credit for rigging up some very fine dwelling places. They had the advantage of time. Their dugouts at Cassino were fantastic. One was so deep that its roof, almost flush with the surface of the ground, consisted of a four-foot layer of dirt and rocks on top, then a section of railroad ties, a thinner layer of stones, a layer of crisscrossed steel rails, and beneath that a ceiling of more thick wooden ties. Its roof indicated that many of our shells and bombs registered direct hits on it, yet I doubt if the explosions even disturbed the sleep of the occupants. The walls were lined with real plywood, nicely fitted, and there were springed bunks which folded into the wall. There was a radio, too, and a number of German magazines. It was easy to see how the krauts were able to snooze blissfully through our worst bombings and shellings, and then come out and fight off our infantry when the big stuff stopped.

The dugout's only weakness was its one entrance—a screen door to protect the delicate krauts from predatory mosquitoes. Cassino was entered by the foot infantry who knocked down the dugout doors with their grenades and bayoneted the occupants. Then our guys occupied the luxurious dugouts for a while.

Those who look carefully at newspaper pictures have probably observed that many Germans are captured at the front without

"No, thanks, Willie. I'll go look fer some mud wot ain't been used."

helmets, while our guys wear them almost all the time. One of the reasons for this is that we were taught very thoroughly that a helmet is a good thing to have around, but the main reason is because the American helmet is a handy instrument even when you're not wearing it. You can dig with it, cook with it, gather

*"Here's yer money back fer them souvenirs. Ya been
scarin' hell outta our replacements."*

fruit with it and bathe with it. The only disadvantage of the
helmet is that it is drafty in winter and hot in summer.

The infantryman bathes whenever he has an opportunity,
which is about twice during the summer and not quite as often
in the winter. He bathes in rivers, seas, and old shell holes which
have collected water. The only consistent thing about his bath is
that it is always cold.

An infantry company in Italy scrounged a real tin bathtub
and they carried it around with them for several weeks until it
was riddled by an 88 shell.

In spite of growing resentment against the souvenir hunter,
the market for souvenirs is booming. Front-line troops pick them

up first-hand, and rear troops buy them or police up what the front-line troops missed. On the local market one hundred bucks is the prevailing price for a Luger pistol. A P-38, the mass-production model of the Luger, will get you about seventy bucks. German helmets are flooding the market and aren't worth picking up.

Shortly after Rome fell, all of the city's better hotels were grabbed by brass hats and the Air Forces. Did the infantry have a hotel? Hell, no. The sightseeing doggie was out of luck if he wanted a place to sleep after he had ogled some of Rome's choicer sights. This was a heck of a note for the doggie who had sweated out Anzio and Cassino and who had pushed north to take Rome after nine awful months in Italy.

It was always a little infuriating for the dogfaces to take a town away from the Germans by dint of considerable effort, to be treated royally by the liberated inhabitants and given the golden key to the city, and, after moving on farther, to come back to that town and find everything changed. All the choice spots are occupied by brass hats and the CIC and AMG and ACC and PWD. All the liquor has been drunk and the pretty babe who kissed the dogface tearfully as he liberated her is already going steady with a war correspondent. It's a bad thing, and even though the doggie realizes all these people have their place in the war, and it is necessary that they follow him, he also gets mad as hell sometimes.

Hence the picture about Joe and Willie being directed to the Catacombs, where Christians used to languish. Whether this sort of cartoon ever did any material good I don't know. I should like to think that the Catacombs drawing inspired some flinty

[163]

*"He says we kin git a room in th' Catacombs. They
useta keep Christians in 'em."*

requisitioning colonel to donate the Grand Hotel to private soldiers in the infantry. But this is a practical world, and if it
happened I didn't hear about it.

Anzio was unique.

It was the only place in Europe which held an entire corps of
infantry, a British division, all kinds of artillery and special
units, and maintained an immense supply and administration
setup without a rear echelon. As a matter of fact, there wasn't
any rear; there was no place in the entire beachhead where
enemy shells couldn't seek you out.

Sometimes it was worse at the front; sometimes worse at the
harbor. Quartermasters buried their dead and amphibious duck

[164]

"My God! Here they wuz an' there we wuz."

drivers went down with their craft. Infantrymen, dug into the Mussolini Canal, had the canal pushed in on top of them by armor-piercing shells, and Jerry bombers circled as they directed glider bombs into LSTs and Liberty ships. Wounded men got oak leaf clusters on their Purple Hearts when shell fragments

"Wisht I could stand up an' git some sleep."

riddled them as they lay on hospital beds. Nurses died. Planes crash-landed on the single air strip.

Planes went out to seek the "Anzio Express," that huge gun which made guys in rest areas play softball near slit trenches. The planes would report the Express destroyed and an hour later she would come in on schedule.

The krauts launched a suicidal attack which almost drove through to the sea. Evacuation was already beginning in the harbor when a single American battalion broke the point of the attack, then was engulfed and died. Bodies of fanatical young Germans piled up in front of the machine guns, and when the guns ran out of ammunition the Wehrmacht came through and was stopped only by point-blank artillery. One American artillery battalion of 155s fired 80,000 rounds of ammunition at Anzio, and there were dozens of these battalions.

You couldn't stand up in the swamps without being cut down, and you couldn't sleep if you sat down. Guys stayed in those swamps for days and weeks. Every hole had to be covered, because the "popcorn man" came over every night and shoveled hundreds of little butterfly bombs down on your head by the light of flares and exploding ack-ack. You'd wake up in the morning and find your sandbags torn open and spilled on the ground.

The krauts used little remote-control tanks filled with high explosives. You wondered how Jerry could see you and throw a shell at you every time you stuck your head up, until you climbed into the mountains after it was all over and were able to count every tree and every house in the area we had held. Tiger tanks grouped together and fired at you. Your artillery thought it was a battery and threw a concentration of shells at the tanks, and by the time your shells struck the Tigers had moved away and were firing at you from another place.

Four American tank destroyers crossed the canal and bounced armor-piercing shells off the turret of a Tiger until it turned its massive gun and disintegrated them with five shells.

German infantry rode their tanks into battle and the dogfaces shot them off like squirrels but they didn't get all of them— some came in and bayoneted our guys in their holes.

This wasn't a beachhead that was secured and enlarged until it eventually became a port for supplies coming in to supplement those being expended as the troops pushed inland. Everything was expended right here. It was a constant hellish nightmare, because when you weren't getting something you were expecting something, and it lasted for five months.

"By th' way, we spotted some kraut gun positions too."

A company of infantry sat on a mountain in Italy in mud, rain, snow, and freezing cold weather. They had inadequate clothing and they didn't get relief. They sat there for weeks, and the only men who came down that mountain were dead ones, badly wounded ones, and those who had trench foot from the icy mud.

During that entire period the dogfaces didn't have a hot meal. Sometimes they had little gasoline stoves and were able to heat packets of "predigested" coffee, but most often they did it with matches—hundreds of matches which barely took the chill off the brew. Soon the guys ran out of matches.

Because they were on K rations they had coffee only once a day. The dinner ration had synthetic lemonade—a mixture of

*"Ya know, I ain't worth a dern in th' morning with-
out a hot cuppa coffee."*

carbolic acid and ersatz lemon powder. Try drinking that in a
muddy foxhole in freezing weather. The supper ration had a sort
of bouillon soup, which was impossible. It takes a lot of water
to make it, and a lot more to drown the salty thirst it causes.
Usually there wasn't even enough water for the guys to brush
their teeth because there weren't enough mules to haul it up.

Our army is pretty well fed behind the lines—as well fed as
an army can be. The food advertisers who show a soldier wallowing in goodies aren't far wrong. The abundance of food in
our big ration dumps amazes Europeans. But the advertisers
make one mistake. They always show the soldier wallowing in

"Drink it all, boys. Th' guy wot put out that order about shavin' ain't comin' up here to inspect us."

goodies at the front. He doesn't wallow in anything but mud up there.

Usually it's nobody's fault. In Sicily and Southern France things moved so fast it was hard for the supplies to catch up. In Italy the mountains complicated the supply situation.

"I caught KP agin."

Since there is not much a cook can do while his company is in combat, his worth depends upon how many ration cases he can carry and not upon how flaky his corn bread turns out. Occasionally a few cooks managed to get hot food up to their boys but this didn't happen very often.

Front-line troops got K and C rations because the bulky B units, which contain fruit juice, flour for pastries, and all the nice things a guy likes to eat, were too much for the mules which had to carry everything else, including ammunition and water. The main trouble with K and C rations was their monotony. I suppose they had all the necessary calories and vitamins but they didn't fill your stomach and you got awfully tired of them.

It's a tragedy that all the advantages of being in the American army never get to those who need them most—the men at the front. It was the same with the Red Cross and movies and all the rest of the better things. You just can't have variety shows and movie screens at the front.

When our planes weren't shooting up kraut supply lines, the German army was pretty well fed. Maybe they didn't know much about vitamins, but their stuff was filling. It was always a great day when our patrols found caches of Jerry food.

Their sausage is good, and they have a marmalade that comes packed in a big wooden box and isn't bad at all. Of course, most of this stuff came from France. Now that they can't get it from the French the German diet will probably get slimmer.

But the Germans have a pretty good chow system, according to prisoners I've talked to. Our guys seldom get a square meal with meat and gravy until they are back in a rest area where the food can be brought up easily. The Germans send all their *best* stuff to the front. One prisoner told me that he had transferred from a cushy job in the rear echelon to the infantry so he could get something to eat.

After having eaten normal German front-line rations, prisoners scream when we throw C rations at them. According to the rules, they are supposed to get the same food as their captors, and they refuse to believe that we also eat C rations.

A captured doggie who escaped and returned to our lines at Anzio reported that he had received three meals a day from the Germans, besides a daily chocolate bar, ten cigarettes, and a bottle of beer. That was a hell of a lot better food than we were getting, and if the krauts fed him like that and then deliberately let him escape, it was a smart trick.

But the kraut wasn't always sleek and well fed. We can thank the fliers and the artillery for the fact that his supplies were shot up a big part of the time. Then he was happy to get black bread and watery soup and didn't object so strongly to C rations if he was taken prisoner.

While the rule books probably frown on it, there are few soldiers who haven't traded army rations for civilian food when it was available. It's funny to watch a civilian, sick of his potato soup, brown bread, and red wine, wolf one of those horrible K rations as eagerly as the soldier tears into the soup and bread and wine.

Every army does some foraging now and then, and I guess European farmers are used to it. In all the Mediterranean areas —especially in Africa and Italy—some of the people more than made up for their losses of fruit, vegetables, and livestock by stealing every piece of army equipment that wasn't nailed down, so they usually got the better end of the deal, as Europeans always seem to do.

The soldiers killed a lot of cows. One rifleman at Anzio insisted that a cow had attacked him and that he had fired in self-defense.

The krauts sometimes used herds of livestock for cover and drove them ahead of the infantry in an attack. Whether the attack was successful or not, both sides usually got fresh meat out of it. A dead cow in No Man's Land sometimes was a major objective for patrol activity.

It's astounding how many soldiers before cleaning their rifles

"I coulda swore a coupla krauts wuz usin' that cow fer cover, Joe. Go wake up th' cooks."

squeezed off a couple of rounds to loosen the dirt in the barrels and a cow just happened to be standing there. Anyone who objected to this sort of thing either didn't like fresh meat or hadn't been living on front-line rations.

One American-Canadian division had a neat system for sup-

"Drop them cans in th' coffee gentle, Joe. We got a chicken stewin' in th' bottom."

plementing their GI chow at Anzio. They dug up German anti-tank mines, wired them electrically, dropped them into the sea, exploded them and then harvested bushels of fish. Such highly unorthodox but extremely effective methods of supply per-suaded the Germans—fearful, perhaps, that having exhausted all

available sources of provision, the dogfaces would turn to canni-
balism—to keep a respectfully wide No Man's Land between
their lines and our own. The boys took advantage of this and
used to run down rabbits and chickens far ahead of our forward
machine-gun positions.

Back in the rest areas kitchens set up mess lines. The men dig
garbage pits and scrape the rust out of their mess gear. The
infantry seems to get much worse food than any other branch,
but at least the food is hot when the troops get back to areas
where the kitchens are functioning.

Those of us who kick around from outfit to outfit know where
to find the best food. That's one of the first things you learn in
the field—to scrounge where the scrounging is best. We know
only too well what the infantry gets.

One of my best friends is a cook in an infantry company when
he's not in the klink. I once drove him back to a ration dump to
get a sack of flour. He wanted to make pancakes for his boys,
who hadn't seen pancakes for seven months. I told the guys at
the ration dump that I was scrounging for *Stars and Stripes,*
and that we wanted to do a story, with photographs, about the
men who work in ration dumps. They fell for it, and didn't even
stop to wonder why in hell *Stars and Stripes* wanted a sack of
flour. We got the sack but those ration men are still looking for
their pictures in the paper.

Halfway back to the company area Mike remembered that we
hadn't asked for baking soda. We went back, but they didn't
have any soda. Then Mike asked for a few cases of tooth powder,
and we got that. After Mike got back to the company, every guy
had all the pancakes he could eat. They were made with GI

"We sure got th' goods on this guy, captain. Civilians wuz supposed to turn in their weapons."

toothpowder, and, in spite of the recipe, they tasted pretty good. That's how the infantry gets along most of the time.

As long as you've got to have an army you've got to have officers, so you might as well make the most of it.

"My, sir—what an enthusiastic welcome!"

The ideal officer in any army knows his business. He is firm and just. He is saluted and given the respect due a man who knows enough about war to boss soldiers around in it. He is given many privileges, which all officers are happy to accept and he is required, in return, to give certain things which a few officers

"Beautiful view. Is there one for the enlisted men?"

choose to ignore. I try to make life as miserable as possible for those few.

An officer is not supposed to sleep until his men are bedded down. He is not supposed to eat until he has arranged for his men to eat. He's like a prizefighter's manager. If he keeps his fighter in shape the fighter will make him successful. I respect those combat officers who feel this responsibility so strongly that many of them are killed fulfilling it.

Since I am an enlisted man, and have served under many officers, I have a great deal of respect for the good ones and a great deal of contempt for the bad ones. A man accepts a commission with his eyes open and, if he does not intend to take responsibilities as well as privileges, he is far lower than the buck private who realizes his own limitations and keeps that rank.

I never worry about hurting the feelings of the good officers when I draw officer cartoons. I build a shoe, and if somebody wants to put it on and loudly announce that it fits, that's his own affair.

A few of them have done it, to the subsequent enjoyment of the guys who read the letters to the editor in the Mail Call section of *Stars and Stripes*. One poor lieutenant—let's call him Smith to be on the safe side—wrote that instead of picking on officers, I should stop and consider the stupid antics of enlisted men whom he had observed in his three years' service. Several letters came back—not defending me, but putting the blast on the lieutenant for being foolish enough to call soldiers stupid. I remember one of the letters very well. It began:

". . . I pick up the October 23rd issue of *Stars and Stripes* and what do I see but a letter from my old pal, Lt. Smith. The last I heard from 'Stinky' Smith, he was studying for his third attempt to make a score of 110 in his General Classification test in order to qualify for OCS. . . . Now, 'Stinky,' when you worked in my poultry house in 1940, picking turkeys for $14 a week, neither myself nor the other boys regarded you as a mental giant. Quite the contrary . . ."

[180]

"Dammit, ya promised to bring rations this trip."

This undoubtedly provided the boys in Lieutenant Smith's outfit with considerable glee.

A very different and very interesting letter was written by a colonel of artillery. He said:

". . . being Regular Army, my father before me, and his father before him, one of the first things I learned at West Point was to respect the enlisted soldier of the United States Army . . ."

The colonel, for my money, is the perfect officer. He is a professional soldier, he likes the army, he likes his job, he likes the men under him, and he knows his business. He carries his rank easily because he is capable of earning respect without ramming his eagles down somebody's throat. I will throw the gentleman

"I wanna long rest after th' war. Mebbe I'll do a hitch in th' regulars."

a salute any time I meet him, and I will look him in the eye while I'm doing it. The army is his home, and while I am in it he is the host whose rules I must respect. In civilian life, if he comes into my home, I am the host, and it is obvious that he is going to be enough of a gentleman to abide by my rules.

I've thrown a drawing or two at the regular army, because too many mess sergeants with thirty years in the army have been made temporary majors and lieutenant colonels, and they are making the most of their moments of glory.

Even after four long years in the army I still disagree with some of the officer-enlisted man traditions. But I'm not rabid about it. If the men who wrote the rules prefer their own exclusive bathrooms and latrines, that's okay with me. But if the

[182]

"Whistle if you see anybody coming."

officer is going to have a tent over his latrine in the field, how about one for me? I might not be as important as he is, but I can get just as wet. And keep him out of *my* latrine when the weather is bad, and his latrine is farther away than mine. If he wishes to eat at his own table, and wants me to wash his dishes

"One more crack like that an' ya won't have yer job
back after th' war."

because he has weighty problems on his mind and no time for dishwashing, then I understand. But let him keep his hands off my own kitchen's canned orange juice.

Many old line officers are no doubt shocked at a spirit of passive rebellion which occasionally shows itself in this citizen army. That's the whole answer. It is a citizen army, and it has in its enlisted ranks many men who in civil life were not accustomed to being directed to the back door and the servant quarters. To taking orders, yes; but to taking indignities, no.

It doesn't hurt us. Nearly everybody needs a little humbling from time to time. If the army maintains these customs to pre-

"Looks like we're goin' into th' line, Willie."

vent undue fraternization between the ruling class and the working class, on the theory that familiarity breeds contempt, then perhaps the army is right. But most combat outfits scrap tradition, as they scrap many other things, when they go into battle. No man who depends upon those below him—not only for his success, but for his very life—is going to abuse his men unnecessarily. Not if he has good sense.

An unpleasant noncommissioned officer can often make life a lot more miserable for the men under him than an officer can, simply because there are certain restrictions on the behavior of officers.

An officer can be court-martialed for calling an enlisted man a son of a bitch, but that, coming from some sergeants who have complete mastery of the army language, can be taken as a small compliment. Also, an officer usually lives a little apart from the boys, so if he says there's to be no gambling, it's easy enough to get a flashlight and hold an exclusive little game under a blanket. But a corporal, bucking for a third stripe, can crawl right in there with you and turn you in if he loses.

The infantry in combat doesn't worry much about rank.

One company I know of had two sets of noncoms for a while. One set led squads and patrols when the outfit was committed. After the company was pulled back to a rest area, this first set lined up to be busted, and an entirely different set—those who had more of an eye for regulations and discipline—took over while the others went out and got tight.

Technicians' ratings have always been good cartoon material. All the boys pick on a technician, but they must call him "sergeant" or "corporal" while they do it.

After I had been a very poor infantry soldier for a year or so, somebody was kind enough to give me an extra cook's rating, which was called a first-third. Although I never saw the kitchen

"Sure I got seniority. I got busted a week before you did."

except when I did KP in it, the rating entitled me to one stripe
and slightly more than corporal's pay. It was a notable occasion
for me, because I got that first-third on my wedding day, and
the few extra bucks did a lot to help me get along with my land-
lady.

"He's already gittin' drunk wit' power."

A few months before I came overseas the rating was changed to "technician, fourth grade." This gave me three stripes and a T, and sergeant's pay. I wasn't doing my company commander any good, because I was on special duty at division headquarters where I drew pictures for the division paper. My peppery little captain used to trudge over to division every day and try to get those new stripes back.

I've still got them, but I don't wear them. I'd rather look like a respectable buck private than take the ribbing most guys give an ersatz sergeant.

In many ways you can compare an MP's problems to those of an officer. For the doubtful privilege of maintaining law and

"They must have infiltrated during the night."

order in the armed forces, and being able to put the cuff on just about anything in uniform, the MP has to take a lot of ribbing— some of it funny and some of it nasty. The smart MP realizes this and accepts it, and the not-so-smart MP lets the ribbers get his goat and finishes his hitch a very bitter man.

"This must be th' joint."

Military cops come in two sizes—combat and garrison. The combat MP is a handy guy to have around, and he is seldom required to be a fanatic about regulations, so he gets along pretty well with the doggies. He has a dirty job because he has to guard crossroads, and anybody who has been around in this war knows what it is to hang around a crossroads within artillery range of the enemy. Being in dangerous places and associating with dog-faces just naturally gives the combat MP the dogface's point of view. If an MP wearing the insignia of the dogface's own outfit tells him something, the doggie usually listens. That's why commanders try to put their own MPs in towns where their troops are raising hell.

The garrison MP is different. He is often unpopular because

"Th' yellow one is fer national defense, th' red one wit' white stripes is fer very good conduct, and th' real purty one wit' all th' colors is fer bein' in this theater of operations."

he has to enforce those garrison rules which we all hate—proper uniform, saluting, passes, and all that sort of thing. When I'm not cussing them I feel sorry for garrison MPs. I feel particularly sorry for them when they are operating under the orders of an unpleasant area commander, because they are the boys who take the rap for him. If the area commander orders that helmets be worn in blazing hot weather fifty miles behind the lines, the MP is the guy who has to stand there and see that helmets are worn, and the soldier is naturally going to place the entire blame for his sick headache on the MP who makes him keep that red-hot piece of steel on his knob.

"Thanks."

Because he picks up a hundred soldiers a day and hears a hundred dirty cracks, none of them original or amusing, the garrison MP is going to be soured on life in general and soldiers in particular, and he is going to become downright mean. Then a peaceable guy like myself is rudely stopped by the MP who asks:

"Where the hell is yer gawdam helmet?"

I start to say truthfully that I forgot it, but he cuts me off.

"Don't you gimme none of yer gawdam lip, dammit—I heard that one before."

This goes on until I get sore and blow my top and he takes me to jail or gives me a ticket, and I go off and sulk and draw pictures about him.

I don't think I ever made a lot of the MPs really sore, except once, when I did the one about the MP way down in his hole at the Anzio crossroads, holding up a wooden hand to point directions. That was no gag. Crossroads are good places to stay in holes—especially Anzio crossroads. The MPs at Anzio told me they liked the picture and sent it home in letters, but I got a round robin from an MP battalion doing garrison and traffic duty at Naples.

"We are getting damned sick and tired of you, Mauldin," the Naples MPs said. "It's bad enough making fun of us, but your cartoon of March 9 called us yellow and insulted the memory of members of the Military Police who have died performing their duty."

I'm really sorry they took it that way, but when I made the cartoon I wasn't thinking of that particular Naples battalion. I don't doubt that many of them, while performing their duty, were run over by trucks and taxis.

It seems to most dogfaces that five minutes after they have stormed and captured a town the whole place is plastered with "Off Limits" signs. Practically every town in France became off limits immediately after our first troops had cleared it of snipers. Sometimes it seemed like the "Off Limits" signs were there to greet the guys when they shot their way into the towns. The doggies weren't bothered too much by the signs, anyway, because they seldom had time to go back to the towns they had taken.

One off limits story spread through the army and endeared General Patch, the army commander, to the doggies. According to the story, Patch picked up a hitchhiking paratrooper down in the Riviera district. The general asked the paratrooper where

"It's either enemy or off limits."

he was going and the paratrooper told him "Cannes." It was off limits and the general told him so. "Hell, that's okay," said the paratrooper. "I can sneak in and nobody will see me until I'm ready to leave." Either the general wasn't wearing his stars on the jeep or the paratrooper didn't give a damn. Anyway, the

"Try to say sumpin' funny, Joe."

general was so impressed with such remarkable honesty that he gave the guy a pass. Patch wrote it out in longhand and instructed all the MPs of his command that the paratrooper was not to be picked up.

It doesn't matter whether the story is true or not. If Patch had been a martinet, nobody would have bothered to repeat the yarn.

"Hope it ain't a rocky beach. Me feet's tender since they got webbed."

You can learn a lot about a general by listening to the stories told about him by his combat men.

Invasions are magnificent things to watch but awful things to be in. Evidently the army likes to pick certain outfits, train them

"You guys oughta carry a little dirt to dig holes in."

in landing operations, and then use the same men for every invasion. This is undoubtedly an efficient system, but it gets a little rough on the guys who do the invading.

My old division was one of several whose only rest seemed to come when they were waiting for boats to carry them to other lands where the language was different but the war was the same. These amphibious creatures have seen so much action that when they land back in the States they will, just from force of habit, come off shooting and establish a beachhead around Coney Island. There they will probably dig in and fight until demobilization thins their ranks and allows the local partisans to push the survivors back into the sea.

A lot of these dogfaces have put in more time at sea than half the men in the navy. These salty infantrymen offer fatherly advice to young sailors on how to tie the bowline and they often correct the seafaring language of the officer of the deck when he calls the "head" a "toilet."

The doggies don't envy the navy. They like its excellent food and dry bunks, but they don't like the cramped shipboard life, and bad as the beach may be, they don't want to stay aboard the ship when the Luftwaffe and the shore batteries start operating. A ship is a hellish big target, and there is no place you can hide.

Once he gets ashore the foot soldier is in his element. He breathes easier, even while he scoops up sand by the helmetful to hide himself.

Beaches are awful when they are being subjected to any kind of fire, because they are always crowded with men and equipment coming off the ships, and the enemy can throw a shell almost anywhere in the area and be sure of getting a hit. Strafing planes are the biggest terror, and the Germans always seem to scrape up a sizable number to make beachheads unpleasant. They played hell with our troops at Sicily, Salerno, and Anzio.

The best invasion I ever attended was that of Southern France. Part of the easiness I felt was the result of being with my old division, and even though nobody knew whether or not the beachhead was going to be tough, the boys were so accustomed to invasions that they didn't spend their time sweating it out on shipboard. It was almost a rest for the division, because before embarking they had put in some pretty tough training to get their sea legs back again. The training was given, ironically enough, at exactly the same spot where the outfit had gone in below Salerno, and one regiment did some climbing exercises on

"I'm lookin' fer turtle eggs, Junior."

the same mountain they had defended more than a year before. Abandoned, rusted landing craft were still bobbing their sterns as the tide changed, and you would find skeletons washed up on the beaches. It was a very grim place and we all lost friends there.

"Now he's gittin' th' fever, Joe. Let 'im edge in a little."

On shipboard we spent most of our time gambling and chewing the fat and leaning over the rail. The weather was swell.

The invasion came off much better than we had expected, with only one division—the one which had been hurt so terribly at Salerno—meeting really tough resistance. The aerial and naval support was far greater than any of the divisions had ever had before. Everything went off according to schedule.

Every drawing in the set of half a dozen or so I made about that·invasion was done before I left Italy. Since it was obvious that we were going to France and that the Germans expected us—but in the wrong place—General Maitland Wilson had a press conference just before the embarkation, and I sneaked in to hear it. After many preliminaries and formalities, General Wilson told his little assembly something they already knew— that they were going to France.

I scrambled back to the *Stars and Stripes* and made up the set of drawings. The editor accepted them with the same air of secrecy as that of a ship's captain receiving his sealed orders. The fact that every Italian on the Mediterranean coast also knew what was coming off did not detract from the solemnity of the ceremony.

I had seen three real beachheads and countless amphibious training maneuvers from Cape Cod to Chesapeake Bay, so I figured the drawings would be quite accurate. But the high brass who arrange such invasions double-crossed me. Any dope knows you can't make invasions unless the dark of very early morning hides your activities. How was I to know that the first wave wasn't scheduled to land until eight A.M.? The first drawing of my series showed the barges going in by the light of flares, and it appeared in Italy about the same time that I was admiring the battered, smoking coast of Southern France from a ship's rail, in the blinding glare of a very high sun.

I got too darn playful with some of my first drawings in Southern France. Even though that campaign was a very fast

"When ya hit th' water swish yer feet around. They kin use it."

one for the first few weeks, it was not an easy war. No war is easy for those who fight it.

The guys were tired from constant marching and they were running into stubborn resistance in spots, but it was such a tremendous change from Italy that their morale was a little better.

"Seen any signs of partisan activity?"

They had expected a tough beachhead, and even tougher mountain fighting. They were very much relieved to find that they could push ahead.

The Maquis and FFI helped a lot, particularly in the mountains. By actually pitching in and helping to chase the krauts

"Tell them prisoners to ack sloppier in front of th'
lootenant. He might start gittin' ideas."

out, the French saved many of their towns from destruction. The French were honestly and sincerely glad to see the Americans come, and the farther north we worked the more hospitable the people became. I had a feeling that we were regarded truly as liberators, and not as walking bread baskets. It was a far cry from Italy.

Some towns actually had street lights and sidewalk cafés open for business and selling real beer, and even though most of the time the doggies went through too fast to enjoy this stuff, it was nice to look at.

I didn't really believe atrocity stories until I had been in France awhile. Now I know why the Germans fight so stubbornly even when they seem to have lost the war. They don't want to take the rap for what they have done.

The Germans know how much the people hate them. When they surrender, most Germans say, "We are regular army—not SS." Maybe they feel a little less guilty.

No actor on earth could have imitated the thorough contempt and disgust and hatred that was on the face of every French child who watched German prisoners march by. And it was awful to see the grief and horror of the bereaved as they forced the Germans to dig up the bodies of their victims and carry them away for decent burial. You never heard the word "Nazi." The word was "Boche" and it was spat out, not as a name but as an epithet.

You can't be expected to believe such stuff until you have seen it. Once you've seen it, you will understand why the krauts preferred to surrender to the Americans, whose women were safe at home.

In Grenoble, a few miles from the Swiss border, I ran into the five soldiers with whom I had shared the difficulties of publishing the *45th Division News* all over the Mediterranean theater, before I went to *Stars and Stripes*.

Every place the *45th Division News* went, screwy things happened and I felt right at home again. We set up our editorial headquarters at Grenoble directly across the street from a regimental command post, and Fred Sheehan used the CP's portable radio to get the latest BBC news for our "Bulletins" column. One of our biggest scoops, courtesy of BBC, informed the astonished men of the 45th Division that Grenoble had just been captured by troops of the American Army.

"Wot's funny about horizontal foxholes?"

Work on the paper was interrupted that first night by reports that a strong force of Germans had appeared on the outskirts of the town. Our French compositors, who were also FFI men, dropped their type sticks and set up machine guns on the street corner. It turned out that an American lieutenant had talked a Jerry major into surrendering a thousand krauts and that the parade was just coming into town. The major was driving a snappy Ford convertible.

All kinds of rumors spring up when troops go a week or so without news. There weren't so many rumors floating around the 45th Division because those boys had a paper. But when I got out to some of the other divisions around Grenoble I heard quite a few rumors. I was told that Hitler had surrendered and

"This is th' town my pappy told me about."

that the United States had started to invade the island of Japan. And I heard that General Eisenhower had been killed by a sniper in London. There were many more stories, but those are a few I remember.

The *Stars and Stripes* mobile unit hadn't yet arrived and the troops needed news. So my five irresponsible companions persuaded me to publish a Grenoble edition of *Stars and Stripes*. I batted out a drawing and the engravers did a rush job. Then I waited until the *Division News* was matted and on its way to press. I borrowed their forms, cut out a few items which were of interest only to men of the 45th Division, added several BBC bulletins and finally gave the stuff to the pressmen. They showed me that I still had one blank page, so I had the cartoon blown up to full page size. I'm still trying to convince a lot of people that this was the only reason I gave myself a full page.

I told the printer to make 20,000 copies of the paper for me and was told that the bill for that many copies would be fifty dollars. I promised payment as soon as the mobile unit arrived but I kept my fingers crossed for I was beginning to have doubts about the legality of the whole business. It just didn't seem right for a cartoonist without any authority to proclaim himself editor and publisher of one of the largest and most respected army newspapers and it was probably wrong to promise payment in government money for such a wildcat project. But by that time the presses were running and it was too late to do anything about it.

Next morning I loaded the 20,000 papers into my jeep and started the long and tortuous ride down the winding roads which lead out of the Alps. I was heading back to Corps Headquarters, a hundred miles away. Every mile or so I'd have to stop and pick up papers which had blown out. The men at Corps received me very well and they distributed the papers to the divisions within a few hours. But when I timidly mentioned the matter of fifty bucks which I had to raise some place, they weren't so enthusiastic. Why shouldn't *Stars and Stripes* pay for its own newspaper? Oh, you published it without any authority? Well, that's a little matter between you and *Stars and Stripes*.

I started back for Grenoble but less than halfway there I was overtaken by a wild-looking crew on a weapons carrier. God save them if it wasn't the entire *Stars and Stripes* staff—everybody in the organization from editors to linotypers and a few officers. Silently I handed over the bill for fifty bucks. I guess they eventually paid it.

"I ast her to teach me to yodel. She taught me to yodel."

When we got back to Grenoble, *Stars and Stripes* began legitimate publication and, for the first time in its long history, sent the paper *back* to front-line infantry troops, for most of the regimental columns were strung out for a hundred miles along the narrow road leading into Grenoble.

"Hell of a patrol. We got shot at."

Two of the drawings I did in Southern France were a little bewildering to the guys who were fighting the same war but didn't happen to be in our area.

The first drawing, the one about the girl teaching the dogfaces to yodel, wasn't too obscure, even if most readers wondered how in hell the dogfaces on patrol ever met such a pretty girl. This, they felt, should happen only in novels.

But the second drawing made everybody in Normandy and Italy who saw it wonder what kind of war I was thinking about when I had a CP set up in a beer garden and a returning patrol griping because they were shot at. Before I drew the cartoon I really did hear a very surprised soldier in just those circumstances complain to an officer that someone had taken a shot at him. But by the time the cartoon reached the troops in Southern France they had settled back into the same old war themselves, and the only guys who got surprised on patrol were those who didn't get shot at.

I offer those two cartoons as proof that anybody with picture-drawing ambitions shouldn't draw war pictures. He will go nuts trying to keep up with the right war at the right time.

Soldiers are very touchy and explosive persons, especially when they are tired from too much combat. That's why people who sit down and write long books about the war can't please all the soldiers, and one innocent sentence or phrase will cause a hullabaloo from the Atlantic war to the Pacific war.

I finished the original manuscript for this book shortly after I returned from Italy to France. Most of it was done in Rome, a city two hundred miles south of the war. I stayed in Rome for a couple of weeks because I wanted to finish some drawings I had sketched in France. I also wanted to sleep in a bed and eat at a table. I did all these things and then picked up the manuscript and read it over. It seemed that I had overstated a few things. Sitting there in a warm room with the sun shining outside, I felt a little worried about the book.

"I hate to run on a flat. It tears hell outta th' tires."

So before I sent it off I went north to think some more about it. Two hundred miles is a long way for a jeep, even such a jeep as my pampered and well-manicured "Jeanie" who had covered more than ten thousand miles of Anzio, Italy, and France. The ordnance people called her the most neurotic jeep in Europe. But they cleaned out the carbon, ground the valves, and adjusted the carburetor. In spite of all this tender care, Jeanie developed ignition trouble on the way north and I had to stop every few miles in a pouring rain and get out and get under. After the first one hundred miles I was very glad the mud had obliterated the name "Jeanie" on the jeep's sides because I was swearing at the car in a way that would have crisped her namesake's lovely ears. I was beginning to forget Rome and get back into the right mood.

I traveled up highway 65 until I reached a battalion medical aid station in an old building nestling under a bluff, seven kilometers above Bologna. Dog company was on top of the bluff and they had 50-caliber machine guns and a mortar OP up there. I parked Jeanie under the bluff because the road right around the corner was raked every few minutes by enemy machine guns.

Inside the aid station, I told the medics I was looking for cartoons, and they waved me to a wooden chair beside a small stove. Because the station and the road around it were under observation and fire, the medics couldn't do business until nightfall, so we played hearts with a greasy deck of cards and made horrible pancakes. We were pretty well protected but once a shell hit near by, and I poked my head out to see if Jeanie was still there.

We were high in the mountains, and there was a heavy fog sliced with rain. The mountain earth had been soaked so it couldn't absorb any more, and the rain made the mud a little thinner and colder.

The doctor was a captain from Florida. He had a young, mournful face and a scraggly blond mustache. He didn't know how to play hearts, so while we played he pestered us with a story about "Old Sport." Old Sport was a dog and he belonged to a pack of bird dogs. Every dog in the pack was a bird dog except Old Sport, but he wanted to go hunting too. The doctor drove us crazy, and then Old Sport became a race horse. Every horse in the stable won races but Old Sport, and he won a few races too.

[213]

"Oh, I likes officers. They makes me want to live till the war's over."

That's silly, but it had us roaring with laughter. After a while a couple of medics started remembering Anzio.

"Were you at Anzio?" one medic asked.

A couple of them hadn't been there.

"Boy, you should have been at Anzio," said a bearded aid man. Then we all started talking about Anzio. Pretty soon the captain said:

"You know where I was during Anzio?"

We told him we didn't know.

"I was in Florida," he said. "Were you in Florida?"

We said no.

"By God, you should have been in Florida," he said. He told

us about amphibious maneuvers in Florida, and he kidded the hell out of us. He was a good egg.

After a while we talked about home. Out came the wallets, and although the captain had a pretty wife and one of the men had a lovely fiancée, Jean's picture carried away honors, but the other two guys were prejudiced, of course, and wouldn't admit it.

I showed the captain a picture of my son, and I said he would be two years old soon and I had never seen him. I looked a little gloomy, I guess, because the doc kidded hell out of me and told me how lucky I was I didn't have to change diapers in Florida.

Down the hill an American gun went rat-tatatat-tat-ta-ta, to the rhythm of "shave and a haircut—two bits," and a German with no sense of humor or rhythm came back with a fast blrrrrrrp.

That reminded us of the war in Italy. We agreed that this was just as miserable and cold and muddy as last winter in Italy, only this winter the Germans seemed to have more artillery.

Then we said that everybody in the States seemed to think the Americans and Germans in Italy were dancing beer barrel polkas and all the war was in France. We thought of a couple of dozen German divisions we were keeping off the necks of the guys in France, and we got a little sore when we remembered how last winter's war in Italy was forgotten.

"Were you in Florida on maneuvers last winter?" the captain started, and we grinned and shut up.

It got dark, and pretty soon some sick guys climbed out of their holes down the hill and came up to the aid station. One had tonsilitis and a fever of 102 degrees. I sat in the corner blowing on the fire and drying the mud on my pants, and watching.

"How would you like to go to the hospital?" the captain asked the dogface. I guess maybe the doggie thought he might be

[2 1 5]

"By th' way, what wuz them changes you wuz gonna make when you took over last month, sir?"

accused of malingering because he said, "I haven't lost anything at the hospital. I wish to hell I hadn't come to the aid station. They need me down at the company."

"There's a cartoon," the captain said to me.

*"Sure they's a revolution in Germany. Git down so they won't
hit ya wit' a wild shot."*

"Hell, nobody would believe it," I said.

"What's the first thing you look for in *Stars and Stripes?*" the
doctor asked the soldier and then turned to grin at me.

"The headlines," said the doggie.

"What's the second thing?"

"Hell, nothing else in the rag is worth reading," said the doggie.

The doctor stopped kidding and examined the doggie. "You're going to the hospital," the captain said. "You've got a fever." The medics fixed up a litter in the corner of the room and put the sick man under blankets.

Pretty soon a guy with a heavy beard and red, sunken eyes came in with a pain in his chest and a deep cough. He had been on outpost lying on a muddy embankment for six days and six nights without being able to stand up or take his shoes off. It had not stopped raining for six days and six nights, and it got below freezing at night and he hadn't had any cover. He didn't have a sleeping bag, and he couldn't have used one anyway, because you can't get out of one quickly if Jerry sneaks up on you with a grenade or bayonet.

He had pneumonia, and while he was waiting for the ambulance to come up to the aid station, I talked to him. He had been overseas three months, and he didn't look any different from the men who had been over three years. He talked a little different, though, because he griped about things which three-year men accept with deadened senses. But despite his griping, he had stayed on that muddy embankment with his eyes open for German patrols until his coughing got so bad his buddies were afraid he would die or tip off the Germans to his position, and so they made him come up to the aid station.

Sometimes the doctor kidded the two sick men and sometimes he was gruff with them, but they knew what kind of guy he was by the way he acted. When the ambulance came up, both men were evacuated to the hospital.

No men came out of the misery and death and mud below us

"We'll be here quite a while, boys. Ya kin take yer shoes off tonight."

unless they were awfully sick. They didn't want to stay down there, but they knew they were needed. They were full of bitches and gripes and cynicism about the whole war, but they stayed, and so they had a right to say anything they pleased.

"I wish to hell I could send every man in every hole back to hot food and a hospital bed with sheets," said the captain, and then he realized he had said something serious, so he made a silly crack to neutralize it.

The little field phone rang. One of the guys in the aid station answered it. It was Charley company with a casualty. The medic took his blankets off the litter he had intended to sleep on, and he carried it out to the medical jeep, which sat in a revetment of sandbags at the side of the building. He asked me if I wanted to go with him. I didn't, but I got up and put on my helmet.

"Now what in hell do you want to go for?" asked one of the Anzio guys I had beaten at hearts. "Haven't you ever seen a foxhole at night before?"

I was grateful to him, because I really didn't want to go. I didn't care if I never saw another foxhole again. But you have to play the game, and so while the two guys were getting ready to go I said:

"Well, you are using barbed wire here, and I guess I ought to see it."

"Haven't you ever seen barbed wire before?" my benefactor asked. Still playing the game, I said yes, I had seen barbed wire before, but well, hell, and I fingered my helmet.

"Besides, there's only room for two in the car with the stretcher in back," he said.

"Well, hell," I said again. "If there isn't any room, there isn't any room. Besides, it's an awfully steep hill." I sat down and took off my helmet. The game was over.

They were back in five minutes, because it was only a thousand yards, and they used the jeep because the hill was steep and the machine was faster than men on foot with a litter. The Germans would have killed the medics just as quickly on foot as with the jeep, if they had felt like killing medics that night. I was glad they got back okay.

The boy screamed as the litter bumped the door coming in.

"Goddam it, be careful," said one of the medics to the other.

They laid the litter on two old sawhorses in the middle of the room, and the bantering, good-natured doctor grabbed the kerosene lantern and went to work. He was strangely different now. His warm, sympathetic eyes got cool and quick and his fingers gently unrolled the bandages, now dark red, which the company aid man had wrapped hastily but efficiently around the wounded man's face. The boys who had kidded and bulled about Anzio and Florida maneuvers and Old Sport were very serious now. One took a pair of surgical scissors and slit through layers of muddy, bloody clothing until the boy was stark-naked in the warm room. His face was a pulp, and one arm and a leg were shattered and riddled.

"God, I'm hurt," he said. "God, they hurt me." He couldn't believe it. His unhurt hand reached for his face and one of the medics grabbed his arm and held it—not roughly, but the way a woman would have done.

"Easy, boy," he said.

"God, I'm hurtin'. Give me a shot," the boy screamed.

"We gave you a shot, Jack," said one of the medics who had read his dogtags and was filling out a slip. "Just a minute, and you'll feel better."

While the doctor and the others worked on the bandages and the splint for the shattered arm, the medic with the pencil said:

"What got you, Jack?"

"God, I don't know. It was a tank. Where's the chaplain?"

[221]

"You don't need the chaplain, Jack," said the medic. "You're going to be okay. What got you? There weren't any tanks around a while ago."

"It was a grenade," said Jack, his hand still reaching for his face. "Where's the chaplain? God, why do you let me hurt like this?"

"How old are you, Jack?" asked the medic persistently. He had already marked "grenade," because the wounds showed that. It had been a German potato-masher grenade, because the holes in his body looked like bullet wounds, but didn't go clear through him, and they weren't as jagged as shell or mortar fragment wounds. Evidently the German had sneaked up while the boy was down in his hole.

Jack said he was twenty years old, he was a staff sergeant, and he was from Texas.

The questioning seemed heartless at this time, but there is a reason for it. If the patient is able to answer, it distracts him from his pain; and if the information isn't gained here, they have to get it back at the hospital.

Jack had guts. Of course he was scared. He knew he was hurt bad, and it's a shock to anybody to get hit. But when they told him he shouldn't reach for his face, he said okay a little sleepily, because the morphine was taking effect.

"Hold a flashlight," the doctor said to me. "The lantern isn't strong enough."

I grabbed a flashlight and held it on the boy while they worked on him. I thought, "Christ, twenty years old!" I felt like an old man at twenty-three. I looked at the holes which had riddled his right arm and practically severed his little finger, and I looked at the swollen bloody gashes on his leg. I looked at his horribly

[222]

wounded face and head, and I thought of how twenty minutes ago he was sitting quietly in his hole wondering how soon he could get home.

I handed the flashlight to the medic who had finished filling out the slip, and I went over to the litter and sat on it with my head between my knees and tried to keep from being sick on the floor.

The medic took the flashlight without even a glance, and nobody looked at me. They went right on working. Pretty soon Jack's face was fixed and it didn't look so bad with a neat bandage and the blood washed off. His arm was fixed in a splint and it looked very neat indeed. He was wrapped up in blankets, and the ambulance came up and took him away. He was full of morphine and probably dreaming of home.

"I don't know what we'd do without morphine," the doc said.

I guess I looked a little foolish and white, and I started to open my mouth. I don't know what I was going to say, but the medic who had taken the flashlight turned to me and said:

"It's funny. I handle these guys every night, and some of them are really in awful shape. But last night one came in not hurt half as bad as Jack and I did the same thing you did."

Another medic said, "We keep some medicine to take care of those things."

They brought out a miracle—a half-filled bottle of Pennsylvania Rye. Now I know damned well one of those guys got that bottle in a Christmas package, and I know he could have sold it for a hundred dollars cash anyplace between Florence and Bologna. Or he could have kept it to himself, and nobody would have blamed him. But we all had a slug of rye—the doc with his

"Do retreatin' blisters hurt as much as advancin' blisters?"

bloody hands and his eyes which were bantering once more, and
the medics who were kidding each other again.

Another sick guy came in. The doc asked him if he had been
at the front, and the guy said, "No, I was three hundred yards
behind it."

"Sir, do ya hafta draw fire while yer inspirin' us?"

Sometimes you can hang around places and guys write cartoon captions for you. I made a note furtively.

I went to sleep on a litter that wasn't being used, and when the odor of coffee woke me up at ten the next morning the aid men told me two more casualties had come in later in the night and that when they picked up my litter and turned it around to make more room I hadn't even budged.

I stayed one more day and one night, and when the fog lifted I poked my head up over the sandbags and peered down the valley that led to Bologna. It looked very peaceful and pretty, because you can't see bullets and there was little artillery during those few hours of light before the fog settled down again.

When there is no fog the country is so nice and clear that you don't show more than your helmet even at the battalion aid station.

I hung around and talked with guys who strayed down from Dog company on top of our cliff. Machine-gunners and mortar men, they were feeling very rear echelon and very sorry for the riflemen in the holes below us. Guys in the holes, of course, were feeling sorry for Dog company, because they could see our cliff getting a pounding from time to time.

A moon came out that night, and I decided not to leave until it got murky again, because I had to cover an exposed stretch of road going back. A cloud came over the moon, and I got into Jeanie and turned around slowly so the motor wouldn't make sparks. Then I started crawling back in very low gear through the cratered and splashy mud. Midway through the open space the motor stopped, and the clouds broke, bathing me in lovely moonlight. I sweated and ground the starter and finally the motor started again.

After I got around the bend I heard a lot of explosions, and I guess maybe they had seen me and threw the stuff too late. Anyway, I kicked hell out of that jeep for the next fifteen or twenty miles.

I felt good when I got back to a building in the rear and, even though I had hardly stuck my nose out from the protection of the aid station sandbags, I felt I had learned something. I sketched sixteen cartoon ideas in three hours.

I came back to Rome, so I could send the book off and finish the sixteen drawings. I read the thing over before I took a bath,

"Wisht somebody would tell me there's a Santa Claus."

and darned if I didn't like it pretty well, even though it may be full of bad grammar. Now I've had the bath and the sixteen drawings are almost finished, and somehow I miss the aid station. It was pretty safe under the cliff, and it was warm and we were able to make coffee. It was full of homesick, tired men who were doing the job they were put there to do, and who had the guts and humanness to kid around and try to make life easier for the other guy.

They are big men and honest men, with the inner warmth that comes from the generosity and simplicity you learn up there. Until the doc can go back to his chrome office and gallstones and the dogface can go back to his farm and I can go back to my wife and son, that is the closest to home we can ever get.